THE MEN IN GRAY

Annotated

Author: Robert Catlett Cave
Introduction by Rex Miller
Edited by Lucy Booker Roper

Annotated Reprint Edition © 2014, Lucy Booker Roper. All rights reserved.

THE MEN IN GRAY
By
ROBERT CATLETT CAVE

NASHVILLE, TENN.
CONFEDERATE VETERAN
Original Copyright, 1911.

The original book is in the public domain. This edition with a new Introduction by Rex Miller, in addition to notes and clarifications constitutes a unique and new intellectual property; therefore this particular reprint edition is © 2014 by Lucy Booker Roper, editor.

To the memory of the men in gray, who, with matchless courage, fought to maintain the principles of the Constitution and perpetuate the Government established by their fathers, and whose heroic deeds crowned the South with deathless glory.

"This book, though small, is *multum in parvo* — a mine of information. I wish it could be read by every man in the North as well as in the South. It ought at least to be in the library of every Southern home." — From Porter McFerrin's review of the book in the "Confederate Veteran Magazine," June 1920, Volume XXVIII. Page 204.

The author, Robert Catlett Cave (1843-1923) was a native of Orange County, Virginia. He was a private in the Montpelier Guard; Company A, 13th Infantry, Army of Virginia. After the war, he became a preacher.

CONTENTS

INTRODUCTION 7

FOREWORD 11

THE MEN IN GRAY 23

A DEFENSE OF THE SOUTH 57

CAVALIER LOYALTY AND PURITAN
DISLOYALTY IN AMERICA 97

APPENDIX: 141

THE CONQUERED BANNER 143

HOW "THE CONQUERED BANNER" CAME TO
BE WRITTEN — AND WAS ALMOST LOST. 145

POEM: "HOW FATHER RYAN'S 'CONQUERED
BANNER' WAS RESCUED FROM OBLIVION,"
BY MRS. J. WILLIAM JONES." 147

INTRODUCTION

IGNORANCE is the lack of knowledge. Revelation illuminates truth in order for one to gain knowledge. Denial of that revelation is stupidity, which is the basis for the oft' used phrase: "you can't fix stupid."

When I was a child I spoke as a child and acted as a child but when I became a man I put away childish things. I was taught to read, study, research, and reason to advance my base of knowledge in order to gain a more sure understanding of history. After all, if you've no idea where you've been you'll certainly entertain confusion over where you are, and will more than likely not have a clue where you are headed. This confusion is childish and certainly unexpected among adults who are presumably "well educated."

Robert Catlett Cave faced stupidity in 1897 following his address honoring the soldiers and sailors of the Confederate States of America in Richmond, Virginia. Just over thirty years after the War Between the States, it became obvious that northern hagiographic academics and spokesmen were intent on obfuscating facts with regards to that terrible and un-necessary war. Their distortion of history became a must in order to deflect from the un-constitutionality of the war as well as the criminality of most of what was accomplished. A conquering army and government will never be charged with war crimes, yet it was and is the stark evidence of their criminal behavior that motivates their academics to this day.

The deification of the 16th President of the United States began immediately upon his assassination by humanist Northern preachers. His Cabinet loathed him and none admired him; but he was the consummate wordsmith and polished his scriptural phrases after his religious debacle early on in Springfield, where not one of the twenty seven Christian Churches supported his grasp for political power. Many of the radical elements including some of his cabinet glommed onto this novel idea in order to distract from the myriad of horrific events that transpired as a consequence of their actions.

Dr. Cave like many other Southern writers was a Christian man; and being Christian believed that truth vindicates. In an honest Christian climate this is certainly true. But in a greedy humanist climate where truth is shouted down by ignorance and nowhere is a fair hearing given, truth suffers. Speaking of Confederate soldiers, Dr. Cave states, "Hence, while they need no one to defend their record as soldiers, they do need to be defended against misrepresentations of their motives and of the cause for which they fought; they do need to have the false and dishonoring accusations of Northern writers and speakers refuted, so that they may appear before the future with undimmed fame."

Now, one hundred and fifty years after that bloody war, we find Americans not only ignorant of the facts but woefully mal-informed of the causes. Truth has been boxed and hidden away in a great government closet and forbidden exposure to the light of day. That truth must be illuminated in order for generations of

Americans to learn where we've been and see where we're headed. No doubt this work of Robert Catlett Cave will illuminate, if you will but read it.

>	Rex Miller
>	Timberville, Virginia

FOREWORD.

WHEN I delivered the oration at the unveiling of the monument to the soldiers and sailors of the Southern Confederacy, in Richmond, Virginia, on May 30, 1894, I supposed that the war was over; that the animosities engendered by it had been buried; that it might be discussed as freely as any other historical event; and that at the dedication of a monument to the Confederate dead a Southerner's attempt to free their memory from reproach by plainly stating the reasons that moved them to take up arms and justifying their action would be received by the people of the North with patience and kindly toleration, if not with approval. However it may have seemed to those who read extracts from it, the speech was not prompted by a malevolent spirit. Indeed, I think I can truthfully say that never, either during or after the war, was I moved by a feeling of enmity toward the brave men who fought under the Stars and Stripes in obedience to what they believed to be the call of duty. I deplored the fact that they had been deceived into taking up arms against what I regarded as the cause of truth, justice, and freedom; but toward them personally I had no feeling of ill will or hostility. I had friends among them—young men of admirable qualities, whom I had met before the war and esteemed highly, and whom I loved none the less because their uniforms were blue.

Not only was I conscious of no feeling of enmity in my own heart, but, so far as I knew, Southern men generally entertained no such feeling. We of the South believed most firmly that the North had unrighteously made war on us; but we credited the Northern soldiers with the same loyalty to honest conviction that we claimed for ourselves, and freely conceded to them the right to speak without restraint in justification of what they had done. We had so far allayed whatever of animosity we may once have felt that we could read misrepresentations of the South and her cause with an indulgent smile, and excuse them on the ground that those who made them believed them to be true.

Knowing this to be the attitude and feeling of the conquered, to whom the war had brought incalculable loss and suffering, I supposed that the conquerors, who had suffered and lost comparatively little, would be equally magnanimous. But I was speedily undeceived. The storm of unjust criticism and bitter denunciation which the speech called forth showed but too plainly that the embers of hate were still smoldering in some Northern hearts, needing but a breath to fan them into flame, and that the time was not yet come when plain speech in justification of the South would receive calm consideration or even be tolerated.

Deeming it unwise and unpatriotic to add fuel to the flame which I had unintentionally kindled, I did not reply to these animadversions; but I think it well to notice here the objection to the speech as a violation of Decoration Day proprieties. In the words of one of my critics: "Decoration Day in both sections belongs to the bravery of the dead. [May 30 has never been Confederate Memorial Day.] Old issues belong to other places of discussion." With this sentiment I am in full sympathy. When we meet where sleep the heroic dead, to pay a tribute of respect to their high courage and soldierly virtues, and, following a custom which originated with the women of the South, reverently to decorate the graves of Federals and Confederates alike, the calling up of the old differences that arrayed them in opposing lines of battle is a gross impropriety. Had I been speaking on such an occasion, I would have raised no question as to whether Federals or Confederates had fought for the right. But the speech was not made on such an occasion. Although delivered on National Decoration Day, it was not at the graves of any dead, but at the unveiling of a monument to the soldiers and sailors of the South. It was a ceremony which pertained not to both sections, but to the South alone—a ceremony in which the Southern people were formally dedicating a shaft that would bear witness to their appreciation of the worth of the men who fought under the flag of the Confederacy and to their desire to perpetuate the memory of those men. Since the highest courage, if displayed in defense of an unjust cause, cannot deserve a memorial, it seemed to me that this shaft was intended to commemorate not only the valor of the Southern soldiers and sailors, but also the righteousness of the cause in defense of which that valor was displayed. Hence I thought it appropriate to speak in justification of their cause, as well as in praise of their courage.

Many Northern orators seem to think it altogether proper to discuss the old differences between the sections, even in the usual exercises on Decoration Day. On the same day that the Confederate monument was unveiled in Richmond Judge J. B. McPherson, as a part of the Memorial Day services held at Lebanon, Penn., delivered an address from which I take the following:

But, while our emotions give this anniversary its peculiar character, we must not forget that its more enduring value lies in the opportunity it affords to repeat and strengthen in our minds the truths of history for which this tremendous sacrifice was made. Our school histories to-day are largely at fault because they do not tell the truth distinctly and positively about the beginning of the war. It is too often spoken of as inevitable. This is not only not true, but it is a dangerous falsehood, because it tends to lessen the guilt of the rebellion and suggests that after all the South was not to blame. I would be the last to deny that a contest of some kind was inevitable between freedom and slavery until one or the other should prevail over the whole nation. But I do deny that an armed conflict was inevitable; I do deny that it was impossible by constitutional means to find a peaceful solution. The solutions which other countries have found for similar problems were surely not beyond our capacity, but the opportunity to try them was refused by the action of the South alone. This, I repeat, was rebellion, and I am willing to call the

Southern soldiers Confederates, since they prefer that title; and while I welcome the dying away of personal bitterness between the soldiers and citizens of both sections, I am not willing to speak of the war as the Civil War or the War between the States, or to use any phrase other than that which the truth of history demands, and that which ought to be taught to every child in our schools for all time to come—the War of the Rebellion. A crime like this, a deliberate attack upon the nation's life, ought not to be glossed over by a smooth turn of speech or half concealed for the sake of courtesy.

The papers of the country had nothing to say of the impropriety of the speech of which the foregoing extracts are fair samples. On the contrary, it was published under double-leaded headlines and declared to be "especially appropriate to the occasion." Here and there in the North speeches containing such misrepresentations of the South are still made on Decoration Day without calling forth any expressions of disapproval from the press. And if it be especially appropriate in the "customary Memorial Day services" to charge that the South refused to give the country an opportunity to find a peaceful solution of the questions at issue by constitutional means, and was guilty of the "crime" of deliberately and causelessly drawing the sword and attacking the nation's life, how can it be especially inappropriate, when dedicating a monument to Southern soldiers, to attempt to refute the charge? Does the propriety of discussing the causes of the War Between the States belong exclusively to Northern writers and speakers?

Did the South, when she laid down her arms, surrender the right to state in self-justification her reasons for taking them up? If not, I fail to see how it can be improper, when perpetuating the memory of the Confederate dead, at least to attempt to correct false and injurious representations of their aims and deeds and hand their achievements down to posterity as worthy of honorable remembrance.

Other comments on the Richmond speech I do not care to notice. In no one of them was there a calm and dispassionate attempt to refute its statements. For the most part they consisted of invective—the means to which small-minded men are prone to resort when they can find no available argument. Apparently this invective proceeded from misconceptions of my meaning, resulting from a hasty and prejudiced reading of what I said; and I am not without hope that, published now with other matter, the speech may be considered more calmly, be better understood, and, perhaps, be more favorably received.

Surely now, when nearly half a century has elapsed since the flag of the Confederacy was furled in the gloom of defeat; when the loyalty of the South has been placed beyond all question by the fact that her sons, in response to the country's call, have fought as bravely under the Stars and Stripes as they once did under the Starry Cross; when, of those who were engaged in the conflict between the sections, all save an age-enfeebled remnant are numbered with the dead; when new men, most of them too young to have taken part in the war and many of them unborn when it closed, have come to the front and are directing the affairs of the nation—surely now our Northern friends will be tolerant and charitable and magnanimous enough to concede to a Southerner freedom of speech in defense of his dead comrades and refrain from heaping abuse on him, even though they may wholly dissent from what he says.

It is said, however, that it is disloyal to maintain that the South was right. Disloyal to what? Certainly not to the existing government. The controversy does not involve any question of loyalty to the government as it now is, but only a question of loyalty to a theory of government which was enunciated by the leaders of the Republican party prior to the war, which, by an unfortunate combination of circumstances, triumphed at the polls and elected its representatives to power in 1860, and the triumph of which led to the withdrawal of the Southern States from the Union. That theory the existing government does not profess to uphold. I believe that no prominent statesman of any party will openly advocate it to-day. Has any President since the war been willing to say in his inaugural address that in shaping the policy of the government in regard to vital questions he would not be bound by the decisions of the Supreme Court? Has any Secretary of State since the war been willing to say that "there is a law higher than the Constitution," and that a pledge to administer the government according to the constitution as construed by the Supreme Court would be "treason?" I think not. The existing government, professedly at least, repudiates that unconstitutional and "higher law" theory. It professes to respect the Constitution as the supreme law of the land. Surely there can be no disloyalty to it in maintaining that fifty years ago the South repudiated and withdrew from the Union rather than accept what it repudiates now.

But is it consistent with loyalty to the existing government to claim that the secession of the Southern States from the Union was not rebellion? Most certainly. The war changed conditions. It established new relations and obligations. It nationalized States that were previously federalized. It changed the union of independent States, held together by mutual consent, into a union of dependent States, held together by national authority. It abolished State sovereignty and changed the federal government, which derived its powers from the States, into the national government, which exercises authority and power over the States. Some things that may not be lawful under the national government established by the war may have been altogether lawful under the federal government that existed before the war. Secession is one of them. To maintain that a State now has the right to withdraw from the Union may be disloyal to the existing national government; but there is no such disloyalty in maintaining that a State had that right under the old federal government, and hence that the secession of the Southern States was not rebellion.

But it may be asked, "Why seek to revive these old issues? What good can possibly result from discussing them? Why not, as a well-known Southern editor puts it, "pay a tribute to the conspicuous valor of the Southern soldiers without a revival of bootless discussions? Why not acquiesce in all that has been said and done and "take up the old, sweet tale of Bunker Hill and Yorktown, and pursue it, under God's blessing, to the end of time? What cause has the South lost which remains to be vindicated or which can be recovered?"

If, as this distinguished editor—somewhat to the discredit of his reputation as a well-informed thinker—affirmed, slavery and secession were the only issues involved in the War between the States, it must be admitted that the South has no cause which remains to be vindicated and has lost nothing that can be recovered. The war abolished slavery, and, with the exception of a few Negroes who found that freedom brought them cares and hardships such as they had not known in slavery, I never heard a Southerner say he regretted it. If the war did not abolish the constitutional right of a State to secede from the Union, it clearly demonstrated that the exercise of that right is altogether impracticable when the Seceders are the weaker party. In the South slavery and secession are dead, and no discussion of old issues can possibly bring them back to life or excite in the Southern heart a desire to restore them.

Nor can a discussion of the old issues add in any way to the rights of citizenship now enjoyed by the Southern people. As the editor quoted above said, in all save pensions, "It is one with the men who followed Grant and with the men who followed Lee. They sit side by side in Congress; they serve side by side in the Cabinet; they have represented the country and are representing it in its foreign diplomatic service with an ability and loyalty which, as between the two, cannot be distinguished the one from the other." The discussion of old difference is not expected to increase the number of Southern office holders, gain for the South any larger share of Federal patronage, cause any inflow of Northern capital to develop her resources and enrich her people, or add to her material wealth in any way whatever. From the viewpoint of one who has an eye for the "loaves and fishes" only, it must seem altogether bootless.

But there are some who do not see in "loaves and fishes" the only thing worth striving for, who think that unsullied honor is better than material wealth, and who are unwilling to prosper and grow fat by acquiescing in perversions of history that tarnish the fame of their heroic dead. In discussing the causes of the war they have no thought of restoring the ante helium conditions of Southern life; they do not aim to recover any material wealth or political place and prestige that the South may have lost; they are not "seeking to raise up a generation of young vipers to undo the good that God has done;" they are not "seeking to make traitors of the fair lads whom we are sending to West Point and Annapolis." Their sole purpose is to state fairly the South's side of the case, to refute the false charge that she plunged the country into a long and bloody war without the semblance of just cause, to bring into prominence the real reason of her withdrawal from the Union, to present her action to the world in a truer and fairer light, and to free her from the reproach which unfriendly and calumnious writers have heaped on her.

I acknowledge to its utmost lawful extent the obligation to heal dissensions, allay passion, and promote good feeling; but I do not believe that good feeling should be promoted at the expense of truth and honor. I sincerely desire that there may be between the people of the North and the people of the South increasing peace and amity, and that, in the spirit of genuine fraternity, they may work together for the prosperity and glory of their common country; but I do not think the Southern people should be expected to sacrifice the truth of history to secure that end.

It has been truthfully said that "history as written, if accepted in future years, will consign the South to infamy"; and only by refusing to acquiesce in it as it is now written can we possibly prevent future generations from so accepting it. By keeping these politically dead issues alive as questions of history, freely discussing them, and reiterating the truth in regard to them, we may possibly counteract to some extent the effect of the misrepresentations found in history as it is now written, add something to the luster of the page that records the deeds of the men and women of the South, and hand their story down to posterity so that their children's children will think and speak of them with pride rather than shame.

With this end only in view and conscious of no feeling of bitterness, I delivered the speech at the unveiling of the monument to the soldiers and sailors of the South. With the same end in view and in the same kindly spirit, I now give this little book to the public. If it shall excite any feeling of enmity in the

North or the least disloyal and traitorous feeling in the South, I shall be sincerely sorry; but if it shall give to any one a truer and juster conception of the South's motives, aims, lofty patriotism, and unwavering devotion to principle, I shall be very glad. R. C. C.

THE MEN IN GRAY.

WHEN I was honored with the invitation to speak on this occasion of the valor and worth of those in memory of whom this monument has been erected, I felt somewhat as I imagine one of old felt when, contemplating the infinite, he said: "It is high; I cannot attain unto it." I keenly felt my inability to rise to "the height of this great argument" and fitly eulogize the soldiers and sailors of the Southern Confederacy.

And yet I felt impelled to speak some word, however weak, in honor of those tried and true men who fearlessly fronted the foe in defense of home and country and battled even unto death for a cause which was dear to my heart while its banner proudly floated over victorious fields, and which I have regarded with an affection sanctified and strengthened by sorrow since that banner was furled in the gloom of defeat.

As death paints our loved ones in softer, fairer colors, and brings us to see as we did not see before

> "Their likeness to the wise below,
> Their kindred with the great of old;"

So the overthrow of the cause we struggled to maintain gave me a still higher appreciation of it and brought me to realize more deeply its oneness with the cause of human freedom in every age and land.

I am not one of those who, clinging to the old superstition that the will of heaven is revealed in the immediate results of "trial by combat," fancy that right must always be on the side of might, and speak of Appomattox as a judgment of God. I do not forget that a Suvarov triumphed and a Kosciuszko fell; that a Nero wielded the scepter of empire and a Paul was beheaded; that a Herod was crowned and a Christ was crucified. And, instead of accepting the defeat of the South as a divine verdict against her, I regard it as but another instance of "truth on the scaffold and wrong on the throne."

> ANNOTATION: Russian General Alexander Suvarov, (spelled various, but similar ways) was never defeated. Suvarov was a crucial general during the First (1768-1774) and Second (1787-1792) Turkish Wars, winning battle after battle. He lived from 1829 (or 1730) to 1800.

Appomattox was a triumph of the physically stronger in a conflict between the representatives of two essentially different civilizations and antagonistic ideas of government.

> "It is a postulate with many writers of this day that the late war was the result of two opposing ideas, or principles, upon the subject of African slavery. Between these, according to their theory, sprang the 'irrepressible conflict' in principle which ended in the terrible conflict of arms. Those who assume this postulate and so theorize upon it are but superficial observers. That the war had its origin in opposing principles which, in their action upon the conduct of men, produced the ultimate collision of arms may be assumed as an unquestionable fact. But the opposing principles which produced these results in physical action were of a very different character from those assumed in the postulate. They lay in the organic structure of the government of the States. The conflict

> in principle arose from different and opposing ideas as to the nature of what is known as the general government. The contest was between those who held it to be strictly Federal in its character and those who maintained that it was thoroughly national. It was a strife between the principles of federation, on the one side, and centralism, or consolidation, on the other.
> —Alexander H. Stephens."

On one side in that conflict was the South, led by the descendants of the Cavaliers, who, with all their faults, had inherited from a long line of ancestors a manly contempt for moral littleness, a high sense of honor, a lofty regard for plighted faith, a strong tendency to conservatism, a profound respect for law and order, and an unfaltering loyalty to constitutional government. Against the South was arrayed the power of the North, dominated by the spirit of Puritanism, which, with all its virtues, has ever been characterized by the Pharisaism that worships itself and is unable to perceive any goodness apart from itself; which has ever arrogantly held its ideas, its interests, and its will to be higher than fundamental law and covenanted obligations; which has always "lived and moved and had its being" in rebellion against constituted authority; which, with the cry of freedom on its lips, has been one of the most cruel and pitiless tyrants that ever cursed the world; which, while beheading an English king in the name of liberty, brought England under a reign of oppression whose little finger was heavier than the mailed hand of the Stuarts; and which, from the time of Oliver Cromwell to the time of Abraham Lincoln, has never hesitated to trample upon the rights of others in order to effect its own ends.

At Appomattox Puritanism, backed by overwhelming numbers and unlimited resources, prevailed. But mere force cannot settle questions of right and wrong. Thinking men do not judge the merits of a cause by the measure of its success. And I believe that the South was in the right; that the cause was just; that the men who took up arms in her defense were patriots who had even better reason for what they did than had the men who fought at Concord, Lexington, and Bunker Hill; and that her coercion, whatever good may have resulted or may hereafter result from it, was an outrage on liberty.

"Might! Sing your triumph songs!
Each song but sounds a shame.
Go down the world in loud-voiced throngs
To win from the future fame.

Our ballads, born of tears,
Will track you on your way,
And win the hearts of the future years
For the men who wore the gray.
All lost! But by the graves
Where martyred heroes rest
He wins the most who honor saves—
Success is not the test.

The world shall yet decide
In truth's clear, far-off light
That the soldiers who wore the gray and died

With Lee were in the right."
—Father Ryan.

I cannot here discuss at length the merits of the Southern cause; but, in justice to the memory of those who died in the struggle to maintain it, I wish to protest against the aspersion that they fought to uphold and perpetuate the institution of slavery. Slavery was a heritage handed down to the South from a time when the moral consciousness of mankind regarded it as just and right—a time when even the pious sons of New England were slave owners and deterred by no conscientious scruples from plying the slave trade with proverbial Yankee enterprise. It became a peculiarly Southern institution not because the rights of others were dearer to the Northern than to the Southern heart, but because conditions of soil and climate made Negro labor unprofitable in the North and led the Northern slave owner to sell his slaves "down South."

With slavery thus fastened upon them by the force of circumstances, the Southern people sought to deal with it in the wisest and most humane way. They believed that the immediate and wholesale emancipation of the slaves would be ruinous to the whites and blacks alike, and that, under the then existing conditions, the highest interests of both themselves and the colored wards committed to their keeping demanded that the relation of master and servant should continue.

But it was not to perpetuate slavery that they fought. The impartial student of the events leading up to the "Civil War" cannot fail to perceive that, in the words of Mr. Davis, "to whatever extent the question of slavery may have served as an occasion, it was far from being the cause of the conflict." That conflict was the bloody culmination of a controversy which had been raging for more than a generation, and the true issue in which, as far as it pertained to slavery, was sharply stated by the Hon. Samuel A. Foote, of Connecticut, when, referring to the debate on the admission of Missouri to the sisterhood of States, he said:

"The Missouri question did not involve the question of freedom or slavery, but merely whether slaves now in the country might be permitted to reside in the proposed new State, and whether Congress or Missouri possessed the power to decide."

And from that day down to 1861, when the war cloud burst in fury upon our land, the real question in regard to slavery was not whether it should continue in the South, but whether the Southern man should be permitted to take his slaves, originally purchased almost exclusively from Northern slave traders, into the territory which was the common property of the country, and there, without interference from the general government, have an equal voice with his Northern brother in determining the domestic policy of the new State. The question was not whether the Negro should be freed or held in servitude, but whether the white man of the South should have the same privileges enjoyed by the white man of the North. It was not the desire to hold others in bondage, but the desire to maintain their own rights that actuated the Southern people throughout the conflict. And it behooves us to insist on this, that the memory of those who "wore the gray" may be handed down to posterity freed from the slanderous accusation that they were the enemies of liberty and champions of slavery, who plunged the country into a bloody war that they might the more firmly fasten fetters on human limbs.

Slavery was no more the cause of the war between the North and the South than taxation was the cause of the war between the colonies and Great Britain. Our forefathers were not so unwise as to impose upon themselves the heavy tax of a war with Great Britain merely to avoid the payment of the comparatively light tax which Great Britain desired to collect from them; and the men of the South were not so foolish as to incur the enormous loss which a war with the North would necessarily bring upon them to avoid the comparatively small loss to which they would be subjected by the non-enforcement of the fugitive slave law and the proposed prohibition of slavery in the territories. What drove the colonies to revolution was not the tax, but the British method of taxation, which violated their chartered rights, denied them political equality with other Englishmen, and menaced the cherished principle of self-government; and what drove the Southern States to secession was not the opposition to slavery, but the Northern method of opposing it, which violated their constitutional rights, denied their citizens equal privileges with the citizens of Northern States in the territories, and threatened such usurpation of power by the Federal government as would deprive them of independence and the right to regulate their own affairs. Not the tax, but the principle of government involved in the method of taxation, caused the revolution; and not slavery, but the principle of government involved in the proposed Northern way of dealing with it, caused secession. The question of taxation brought the deeper question of governmental principle to the front in the one case, and the question of slavery brought the deeper question of governmental principle to the front in the other case.

And it also behooves us, in justice to the men who served under the banner of the Confederacy, to insist that they were not rebels fighting against lawful authority and seeking to destroy the Union formed by the fathers of American independence. That Union was dear to the hearts of the Southern people. They regarded it as a fraternal federation founded in wisdom and patriotism, and in no case were they disloyal to the obligations which it imposed upon them.

The impartial student of American history will find that the sons of the South were always among the foremost in the battles of the Union against foreign foes, and that they were ever readiest to make sacrifices in the interest of harmony between the sections.

For the sake of maintaining the Union the South made concession after concession, surrendered right after right, submitted to unjust taxation, consented to compromises every one of which tended to weaken herself and strengthen the North, and for more than forty years clung to the national compact in flagrant violations of its spirit and letter by Northern men.

If history affords an instance of loyalty to an established form of government more unswerving and self-sacrificing than that of the Southern people to the Union, I fail to recall it. Mr. Davis voiced the feeling of the South when he said in the Senate chamber: "If envy and jealousy and sectional strife are eating like rust into the bonds our fathers expected to bind us, they come from causes which our Southern atmosphere has never furnished. As we have shared in the toils, so have we gloried in the triumphs of our country. In our hearts, as in our history, are mingled the names of Concord and Camden and Saratoga and Lexington and Plattsburg and Chippewa and Erie and Moultrie and New Orleans and Yorktown and Bunker Hill." Had the South loved the Union less and clung to it less tenaciously; had she refused to make concessions and sacrifices for its preservation; had she, instead of weakening herself by compromises for its sake, withdrawn from it when first her rights were assailed, the pen of the historian would never have recorded the story of Appomattox. It was her attachment to the Union—her unselfish loyalty and patriotism—which caused her so long to endure Northern aggression, yield again and again to Northern demands and place herself in a position in which her defeat was possible.

But the Union which the men of the South loved, and which they were willing to make concessions and sacrifices to perpetuate, was that formed by the fathers "to establish justice, insure domestic tranquillity, provide for the common defense, promote the general welfare, and secure the blessings of liberty." It was a fraternal federation of sovereign States, guaranteeing equal rights to all and leaving each free to regulate its domestic affairs in its own way. It was a union in which, in reference to questions of foreign policy, every citizen would echo the sentiment expressed by Patrick Henry when, after Concord and Lexington, in a message to Massachusetts, he said: "I am not a Virginian; I am an American." And yet it was a union in which, in reference to questions of domestic policy, every citizen, like that same great orator and patriot, would recognize the right of his own State to his highest allegiance. It was a union in which the people of each State would enjoy the blessings of local self-government and find in "home rule" a safeguard against any possible attempt of the Federal power to interfere with their peculiar interests.

When it became evident that this Union was to exist in name only; when its essential principles had been overthrown and trampled in the dust; when the spirit of fraternity had given place to a bitter feeling of sectional hostility; when New England speakers and writers were heaping abuse and slander upon the South and teaching the people that they "would be poor children of seven years' disobedience to laws" if they supposed that they were obliged to obey the law of the land which protected the Southern people in the peaceful possession of their institutions; when the men of the North, instead of permitting the South to enjoy that domestic peace and tranquillity which the

Union was intended to secure to every section of the country, were persistently striving to stir up insurrection in the Southern States and glorifying those who attempted to carry outrage and massacre into Southern homes; when the tendency to centralization was threatening to destroy State independence and build on its ruins a despotism akin to that which enslaved France when it was said that "the government was sent down to the subject provinces by mail from Paris, and the mail was followed by the army, if the provinces did not acquiesce;" when the reins of government had passed into the hands of a purely sectional party avowedly hostile to Southern interests and declaring the Constitution to be "a covenant with death and a league with hell" which ought to be supplanted by a so-called "higher law"—in a word, when it became evident that Northern power was to sit on the throne in Washington and make the Yankee conscience rather than the Constitution the fundamental law of the land, the Southern people felt that the preservation of community independence and liberty, won at Yorktown and bequeathed to them by their fathers as an inalienable birthright, demanded the resumption of the powers intrusted by them to the Federal government.

Not as a passion-swept mob rising in mad rebellion against constituted authority, but as an intelligent and orderly people, acting in accordance with due forms of law and within the limit of what they believed to be their constitutional right, the men of the South withdrew from the Union in which they had lived for three-fourths of a century, and the welfare and glory of which they had ever been foremost in promoting.

They did not desire war, nor did they commence the war. It is true that they fired the first gun; but every one who is familiar with the history of those stormy days knows that the North committed the first overt act of war, which justified and necessitated the firing of that gun.

Instead of meeting the issues of the hour frankly and honestly, showing a disposition to treat the North and the South with equal fairness, adopting conciliatory measures, and using every possible means of effecting an amicable adjustment of the differences between the sections, as a wise statesman desirous of peace would have done, President Lincoln, influenced by his advisers perhaps, adopted a policy which made war inevitable. While professing to seek peace, he secretly provoked war. While his Secretary of State, Mr. Seward, was giving the representatives of the South most positive assurances that Fort Sumter would be speedily evacuated, he was secretly making preparations to strengthen and hold it. When these preparations had been completed and "transports and vessels of war, with troops, munitions, and military supplies," had sailed from Northern ports and been given time to reach the vicinity of Charleston, he notified the Governor of South Carolina that Sumter, instead of being evacuated in accordance with the explicit pledge of Mr. Seward, would be supplied, and that force would be used if necessary. "The notice," as Mr. Greg justly says, "was a declaration of war—the dispatch of the expedition the commencement of active hostilities." It placed the Confederates in a position in which they were compelled either to silence the guns of Sumter or expose themselves to the combined fire of the fort and the fleet on the arrival of the latter.

But, notwithstanding the deception that had been practiced upon them and the now declared hostile intention of the government at Washington, they were unwilling to resort to violence without a still further effort to maintain peace. They offered to abstain from opening fire upon the fort if its commander would say when he would surrender it and agree not to use its guns against them in the meantime. Major Anderson's reply to this offer, while most courteous in tone and expressive of an earnest "desire to avoid the useless effusion of blood," was such as to leave no doubt that he would use his guns against them in case of any hostile act on their part against the flag of his government—in other words, in case they should offer any resistance to the fleet that was approaching. The Confederates, therefore, could not consistently with the demands of prudence and safety do otherwise than reduce the fort.

Referring to this action of the Confederates, Mr. Davis says: "The forbearance of the Confederate government under the circumstances is perhaps unexampled in history. It was carried to the extreme verge, short of a disregard of the safety of the people who had intrusted to that government the duty of their defense against their enemies. The attempt to represent us as the aggressors in the conflict which ensued is as unfounded as the complaint made by the wolf against the lamb in the familiar fable. He who makes the assault is not necessarily he that strikes the first blow or fires the first gun. To have awaited further strengthening of their position by land and naval forces, with hostile purpose now declared, for the sake of having them 'fire the first gun' would have been as unwise as it would be to hesitate to strike down the arm of the assailant who levels a deadly weapon at one's breast until he has actually fired. . . . After the assault was made by the hostile descent of the fleet, the reduction of Fort Sumter was a measure of defense rendered absolutely and immediately necessary. . . . Even Mr. Horace Greeley, with all his extreme partisan feeling, admitted that, 'whether the bombardment and reduction of Fort Sumter shall or shall not be justified by posterity, it is clear that the Confederacy had no alternative but its own dissolution.'"

The Northern people generally, not knowing the facts in the case, regarded the attack on Sumter as an insult to their flag and an unprovoked and atrocious act of hostility to their government. The Northern heart, which had not been altogether ready to engage in fratricidal strife, was thoroughly inflamed, and fully prepared for war by the fact that the South had "fired on the flag."

This, if we may accept a statement made by the New York Herald a few weeks later, was what Mr. Lincoln and his advisers desired, what they had planned and worked for. In its issue of the 11th of May that paper, which was supposed to be careful and accurate in its statements, said: "The demonstration which precipitated the attack on Fort Sumter was resolved upon to prove to the country and the world the true character and object of the rebellion. It was, in fact, the first tangible evidence we had that the government had a policy, and the success with which it has been attended has inspired more confidence in its ability to carry us through our present difficulties." But a policy cannot be rightly termed successful unless it accomplishes its object. Hence if the policy of making a demonstration against Charleston was "attended" with "success," as the Herald declared, its real object must have been, not to relieve Sumter, but to force the Confederates into an act of hostility which would inflame the North and destroy any sentiment in favor of peace that might exist there. The relief of Sumter was only a pretext for a "silent aggression, with the object of producing an active aggression from the other side," that would incite the Northern people to invade the South with fire and sword. This view of the matter, which is strongly supported by the facts, justifies the assertion that Mr. Lincoln and his advisers deliberately "forced the South and tricked the North into war." Verily "the times were great and the men were small."

They made every effort consistent with their safety, self-respect, and manhood to avert war. They parted from their Northern brethren in the spirit in which Abraham said to Lot: "Let there be no strife, I pray thee, between me and thee."

But the North would not have it so. Every proposal looking to peace was rejected by those in power at Washington. Says an English historian of the time:

"Twice the Republicans were asked simply to execute the existing law and sustain in the future that exclusive constitutional right of the States over their internal affairs and that equality in the common territories which scarcely admitted of rational dispute; and twice the party pronounced against the least that the South could safely or honorably accept."

At length, on April 15, 1861, the newly inaugurated President, transcending the authority vested in him by the Constitution which he had just sworn to support, issued a proclamation calling for seventy-five thousand men to coerce the States which had withdrawn from the Union.

In 1832, when it was thought by some that the President would employ the military to enforce the law in South Carolina, Daniel Webster in a speech at Worcester, Mass., said: "For one, sir, I raise my voice beforehand against the unauthorized employment of military power and against superseding the authority of the laws by an armed force under pretense of putting down nullification. The President has no authority to blockade Charleston; the President has no authority to employ military force till he shall be duly required so to do by law and by the civil authorities. His duty is to cause the laws to be executed. His duty is to support the civil authority. His duty is if the laws be resisted to employ the military force of the country if necessary for their support and execution; but to do all this in compliance only with law and with decisions of the tribunals."

On March 15, 1861, Stephen A. Douglas, in support of a resolution favoring the withdrawal of United States troops from Southern forts, said:

> But we are told that the President is going to enforce the laws in the seceded States. How? By calling out the militia and using the army and navy! These terms are used as freely and flippantly as if we were in a military government where martial law was the only rule of action and the will of the monarch was the only law to the subject. Sir, the President cannot use the army or the navy or the militia for any purpose not authorized by law, and then he must do it in the manner, and only in the manner, prescribed by law. What is that? If there be an insurrection in any State against the laws and authorities thereof, the President can use the military to put it down only when called upon by the State Legislature, if it be in session, or, if it cannot be convened, by the Governor. He cannot interfere except when requested. If, on the contrary, the insurrection be against the laws of the United States instead of a State, then the President can use the military only as a posse comitatus in aid of the marshal in such cases as are so extreme that judicial authority and the powers of the marshal cannot put down the obstruction. The military cannot be used in any case whatever except in aid of civil process to assist the marshal to execute a writ.... Then, sir, what cause is there for apprehension that the President of the United States is going to pursue a war policy unless he shall call Congress for the purpose of conferring the power and providing the means? I presume no Senator will pretend that he has any authority under the existing law to do anything in the premises except what I have stated and in the manner I have stated.... But it may be said that the President of the United States ought to have the power to use the military to enforce the law. ... Be that as it may, the President of the United States has not asked for that power. He knew that he did not possess it under the existing laws, for we are bound to presume that he is familiar with the laws which he took an oath to execute.

That Mr. Webster and Mr. Douglas understood and correctly stated the law in the case cannot be denied. Yet, while the President of the United States could not lawfully employ military force except "in compliance with decisions of the tribunals," as Mr. Webster declared, and except "in aid of civil process to assist the marshal to execute a writ," as Mr. Douglas declared, President Lincoln, without waiting for the decision of any tribunal, without any civil process, without any writ to execute or any marshal in the South to execute it, called for a military force of 75,000 men to invade the Southern States and put down an alleged insurrection. He thus violated the law which his oath of office required him to execute and assumed the power of an autocrat. But for this unlawful procedure there would probably have been no war.

It is claimed that this action of the President was justified by the fact that the South had "fired on the flag." On this point it is proper to note the fact that on a former occasion the Northern people did not regard firing on the flag as an offense sufficient to justify a lawful call for the militia to invade the Offender's territory. In 1807 a British man-of-war fired on an American frigate, killed and wounded several of her crew, compelled her to strike her colors, carried off four of her sailors, and hung one of them. The people of New England did not think that this outrage called for any hasty action by the President against Great Britain. On the contrary, when, some years later, after outrage upon outrage had been added to this and all peaceful means of obtaining redress had failed, war was declared by Congress and the President called for the militia in a lawful way, New England protested against the action of the government as exceedingly wicked. And if firing on the flag when it floated over the Chesapeake, in which Great Britain had not a semblance of right, did not justify a lawful call for the militia to resent the insult, how could firing on the flag when it floated over Sumter, to which South Carolina did have some right, justify an unlawful call for the militia to resent it? Was it greater love for the flag or greater hate for the South that wrought this change in New England sentiment? I am constrained to think it must have been the latter when I recall the following lines [written in 1854] which, if I mistake not, expressed the feeling of a goodly number of the people of New England a few years before the war:

> "Tear down the flaunting lie,
> Half-mast the starry flag!
> Insult no sunny sky
> With hate's polluted rag."

NOTE: The above lines, often mistakenly attributed to Horace Greeley, were actually written by Irish immigrant journalist, author, and poet, Charles Graham Halpine (1829-1868). The reason Halpine wrote this poem was because he was very angry at that time with the United States Government and President Franklin Pierce. The government had returned (at government expense) a runaway slave, Anthony Burns (who was living in Boston) to Virginia in 1854 under the auspices of the Fugitive Slave Act. The poem reflected the sentiment of many, especially in the Northeast. Halpine, who sometimes wrote under the nom de plume, "Private Miles O'Reilly," would later accompany Gen. David Hunter as a staff-

officer on the expedition that wreaked havoc on the Shenandoah Valley in the spring of 1864. See the Appendix for the full poem. (Source of Information: "Reminiscences of James A. Garfield," by Corydon Eustathius Fuller. Cincinnati: Standard Publishing Company, 1887, page 164-169.)

In the estimation of these people, the flag was a "flaunting lie" and a "polluted rag" when it represented the fulfillment of constitutional guarantees to the Southern people; but when it represented an infringement of the constitutional rights of the South, it became "Old Glory," an insult to which must be quickly resented, even in defiance of the law.

But even if firing on Sumter, instead of being deliberately provoked, had been an unprovoked outrage, it would not have justified unlawful means of punishing or redressing it. The theory that we may unlawfully punish lawlessness and enforce obedience to law is the theory of the lyncher. The enforcement of law which cannot be effected without violating law is itself unlawful, and the fact that the Federal government could not coerce the Southern States without trampling the law of the land in the dust proves that the coercion was unconstitutional and an outrage.

This call for troops destroyed the last lingering hope of peace. It left no doubt as to the purpose of the party in power. It meant a war of invasion and subjugation. It left the South no choice but between cowardly surrender of rights held sacred and manly resistance to the invading foe. Between these alternatives she was obliged to choose. States which had been hesitating on the ground of expediency, hoping for a peaceable adjustment of issues, wheeled into line with the States which had already seceded. Virginia, mother of States and statesmen and warriors, who had given away an empire for the public good, whose pen had written the Declaration of Independence, whose sword had flashed in front of the American army in the war for independence, and whose wisdom and patriotism had been chiefly instrumental in giving the country the Constitution of the Union—Virginia, foreseeing that her bosom would become the theater of war, with its attendant horrors, nobly chose to suffer rather than become an accomplice in the proposed outrage upon constitutional liberty. With a generosity and magnanimity of soul rarely equaled and never surpassed in the history of nations, she placed herself in the path of the invader, practically saying, "Before you can touch the rights of my Southern sisters, you must cut your way to them through my heart."

From the Potomac to the Gulf, from the Atlantic to the Rio Grande the sons of the South sprang to arms. From stately mansion and from humble cottage, from the workshop and from the farm, from the storeroom and from the study, from every neighborhood and from every vocation of life, with unanimity almost unparalleled, they rallied for the defense of the land they loved and of what in their inmost souls they felt to be their sacred and inalienable birthright.

Traitors and rebels verily they were not. They were true-hearted patriots, worthy to rank with the noblest souls that ever battled for freedom. They fought for home and country and to maintain the fundamental principle of all free government—that the right to govern arises from and is coexistent with the consent of the governed.

And if patient self-denial and cheerful self-sacrifice and fortitude and unfaltering devotion to country and unwavering loyalty to duty and dauntless courage in defense of the right make heroism, the men whom we honor to-day, and whom we would not have our children forget, were sublime heroes. History has no more illustrious page than that which tells of their achievements. Poorly equipped, poorly clad, poorly fed, and virtually without pay, they confronted more than three times their number of as well-equipped, well-clothed, well-fed, and well-paid soldiers as ever marched to battle, wrested from them a series of victories unsurpassed in brilliancy, and for four years, stormy with the red blasts of war, successfully resisted all their power. In dangers and hardships that "tried men's souls" the defenders of the South were tried and always found "true as tempered steel." Laboring under disadvantages which even their friends can never fully appreciate, supplementing their scanty rations with weeds and grasses, their bare feet often pressing the frozen ground or blistered on the burning highway, their garments as tattered as the battle torn banners that they bore, they bravely fought on for the cause they loved and sealed their devotion to it with their blood.

I need not name the many glorious fields on which the soldiers of the Confederacy, by their splendid courage, hurled back army after army, each one outnumbering them and supposed by the North to be strong enough to crush them. I need not recount the battles in which the sailors of the Confederacy made up in skill and daring for lack of equipment and fought with a valor unsurpassed in naval warfare. On the land and on the sea they made a record to which their country may point with a just and noble pride. History bears witness to their unrivaled martial qualities. By their deeds they "set with pearls the bracelet of the world" and won for themselves a place in the foremost rank of mankind's Legion of Honor. And although, worn out by ceaseless conflict, half famished, and overwhelmed by numbers, they were at last forced to yield; those to whom they surrendered might well envy the glory of their defeat.

And the glory of that great struggle for constitutional liberty and "home rule" belongs not alone to those who wore the officer's uniform and buckled on the sword, but as well to those who wore the coarser gray of the private and shouldered the musket. We do well to honor those who served in the ranks and faithfully and fearlessly performed the duties of the common soldier or sailor. It was their valor and worth, no less than the courage and genius of the officers who led them, that won for the battle flag of the South a fame which:

". . . on brightest pages
Penned by poets and by sages,
Shall go sounding down the ages."

(Lines from the "Conquered Banner," by Father Abram Ryan. See the Appendix for the full poem and how it came to be written. —Ed.)

In education, intelligence, and thought they were from training and associations far above the average soldiery of the world. Notwithstanding all that has been said about the illiteracy of the South, I believe that no country ever had a larger percentage of intelligent and thinking men in the ranks of its army. Thousands of them were highly educated, cultured, refined, and in every way qualified to command. Sitting on the brow of the mountain overlooking the winding Shenandoah and the little town of Strasburg and the beautiful valley stretching away toward Winchester, at that time dark with the blue columns of Federal soldiers, a Louisiana private, idly talking of what he would do were he in command, gave me almost every detail of the plan which, afterwards perceived and executed by the commanding officer, carried confusion and defeat to the Federals. Had the need arisen, as in the case of the Theban army in Thessaly, more than one Epaminondas might have been found serving as a private in the Confederate ranks.

ANNOTATION: Epaminondas, Greek: circa 418 – 362 BC), was a Theban military leader and statesman of the 4th century BC who changed the Ancient Greek city-state of Thebes, bringing it from the days of Spartan suppression into a dominant place in Greek politics.

And I believe that no army was ever composed of men more thoroughly imbued with moral principle.

With comparatively few exceptions, they were men who recognized the obligation to be just and honest and merciful and to respect the rights of others even in time of war. Never flinching from conflict with armed foemen, their moral training and disposition forbade them to make war upon the weak and defenseless. To their everlasting honor stands the fact that in their march through the enemy's country they left behind them no fields wantonly laid waste, no families cruelly robbed of subsistence, no homes ruthlessly violated. "In no case," says an English writer, "had the Pennsylvanians to complain of personal injury or even discourtesy at the hands of those whose homes they had burned, whose families they had insulted, robbed, and tormented. Even the tardy destruction of Chambersburg was an act of regular, limited, and righteous reprisal." The Pennsylvania farmer whose words were reported by a Northern correspondent paid the Southern troops a merited tribute when he said, "I must say they acted like gentlemen, and, their cause aside, I would rather have forty thousand rebels quartered on my premises than one thousand Union troops."

And they acted like gentlemen not merely because the order of the commanding general required them so to act, but because the spirit within them was in harmony with and responded to that order. In the ranks of the Southern army, uncomplainingly and cheerfully performing the duties of the humble soldier, with little hope of promotion when intelligence, ability, and daring were so common, were men

> "True as the knights of story,
> Sir Launcelot and his peers."

And these humble privates no less than their leaders deserve to be honored. It was Jackson's line of Virginians rather than Jackson himself that resembled a stone wall standing on the plains of Manassas while the storm of battle hissed and hurtled and thundered around them. And if I mention the name of Jackson rather than that of the ruddy-faced boy who fell, pierced through the brain, and was buried on one of Virginia's hills, in a lonely grave over which to-day the tangled wild weeds are growing, it is not because the one was more heroic than the other, but because Jackson, by his greater prominence, more fully embodies before the eyes of the world the patriotism and courage and heroism that glowed no less brightly and steadily in the heart of the beardless boy. These noble qualities, possessed by both and displayed by each as his ability and position permitted, bind them together in my thought, not as officer and private, but as fellow-soldiers and brother patriots. Exalted virtue, like deepest shame, ever obliterates rank and brings men into a common brotherhood.

As my mind recalls the persons and events of those years in which the Confederacy struggled for life, there rises before me the majestic figure of the great Southern chief—the peerless soldier and the stainless gentleman; the soldier who was cool, calm, and self-possessed in the presence of every danger, and who, with marvelous foresight and skill, planned masterly campaigns, directed the march of war, ruled the storm of battle, and guided his men to victory on many a well-fought field; the gentleman who was as pure as a falling snowflake, as gentle as an evening zephyr, as tender as the smile of a flower, and as patient as the rock-ribbed mountains. I need not name him, for his name is written in ever-enduring letters on the heart of the South and honored throughout the civilized world. Around him I see a company of intrepid leaders whose achievements have surrounded their names with a glory which outshines the luster of coronets and crowns. I would not pluck one leaf from the laurel with which they are garlanded. I would, if I could, lift to a still higher note and sing in still loftier strains the paeans that are chanted in their praise. But I see also the men whom these noble captains led—men unswerving in their devotion to a noble purpose, self-forgetful in their fidelity to what they saw to be right, and sublimely self-denying and self-sacrificing in their adherence to the cause they espoused; men who loved their country with a love stronger than the love of life, and who, with no thought of compensation beyond that country's freedom and honor and safety, bravely toiled and suffered and endured and gave their bodies to be torn by shot and shell, and shed their blood like water to the thirsty ground. And with uncovered head and profoundest reverence I bow before those dauntless heroes, feeling that, if the greatest suffering with the least hope of regard is worthy of the highest honor, they deserve to stand shoulder to shoulder with Lee and his lieutenants in the brotherhood of glory.

They are honored by all the true and brave who have heard the story of their valiant struggle. Courageous self-sacrifice resulting from honest conviction of duty touches an answering chord in all manly hearts. The heroic soul greets all heroes as kindred spirits, whether they are found fighting by its side or leveling lance against it. It is the narrow, ungenerous, and selfish soul that can find nothing to admire in the courage, devotion, and heroism of its enemies. Hence the Northern writers who have disparaged and ridiculed the valor and devotion of the Southern troops have shown themselves to be wanting in true nobility. In vain have they sought to dim the fame of the Confederate warriors. That fame will emblaze the pages of history when they and all that they have written shall have perished from the memory of man.

> Though the earth
> Forgets her empires with a just decay,
> The enslavers and the enslaved, their death and birth;
> The high, the mountain majesty of worth
> Should be, and shall, survivor of its woe,
> And from its immortality look forth
> Into the sun's face, like yonder Alpine snow,
> Imperishably pure above all things below.

The above lines are from Lord Byron's Childe Harold's Pilgrimage, Canto III, Stanza lxvii. —Editor.

Yes, the high, majestic worth of the Confederate soldiers and sailors shall be "survivor of its woe," and, surviving, shall help to lift the world into higher life. Although they were defeated, their struggle was not in vain. In the world's life wrong has often triumphed for a season. There have been many times of oppression when human rights were trampled in the dust by despotic power and the hopes of men seemed dead. But the student of history will find that every chaos has been followed by a cosmos. The agony and sweat and tears and blood of every age have brought forth a new and better era.

And reasoning from what has been to what shall be, I believe that not in vain were the battles and not in vain was the fall of those who battled and fell under the banner of the Confederacy. Having by their glorious deeds woven a crown of laurel for the brow of the South that drew to her the admiring mind of the world, by their fall they entwined in that crown the cypress leaves that draw to her the sympathizing heart of the world. The land in which we live is dearer to our hearts since it has been hallowed by their sacrifices and watered with their blood. Though dead, they still speak, admonishing us to prove ourselves worthy of kinship with them by being heroes in peace as they were heroes in war. In our country "the war drum throbs no longer, and the battle flags are furled." The quiet stars that, thirty years ago, looked down on sentineled camps of armed and march-wearied men, resting for the morrow's conflict now look down night after night on quiet homes where the sleepers, disturbed by no call to arms, peacefully slumber until singing birds wake them to the bloodless labors of a new-born day.

Fields that were clouded by the smoke of battle and trampled by charging thousands and torn by the hoof beats of the war horse and plowed by the shot of cannon and drenched with the blood of dead and mangled men are now enriched by tillage and contributing their fruits to sustain the life and increase the wealth of the people. "Peace folds her wings over hill and valley."

But peace as well as war demands of us high devotion and unswerving loyalty. If with peace we have decay of patriotism and loss of virtue and the triumph of private over public interests and the sacrifice of law and justice to secure partisan ends—if with peace we have the accumulation of wealth at the cost of the country's welfare and the honest manhood of its citizens, that peace must prove but the slippery, downward path to the ruin in which so many nations, once great and prosperous, have been swallowed up. Better far the desolations and horrors of war than such peace.

From such peace—peace joined with corruption and enjoyed at the expense of true and noble manhood—the soldiers and sailors of the Confederacy, speaking through this monument of their self-sacrificing and heroic devotion, shall help to save our land. Their spirits, glory-crowned, hover over us and beckon us on in the paths of patriotism and honor. Their example bids us nobly live for the principles for which they bravely fought and died*—the principles of State sovereignty and home rule on which this government was wisely founded by our fathers, without which no vast territory like ours can possibly remain democratic, departure from which is rapidly hurrying the country to a choice between anarchy and imperialism, and return to which is essential to the preservation of the life of the republic.**

>*So, you see, my opinion is that the cause which was lost at Appomattox C. H. was not the federative principle upon which American free institutions were based, as some have very erroneously supposed. This is far from being one of the results of the war. The cause which was lost by the surrender of the Confederates was only the maintenance of this principle by arms. It was not the principle itself that they abandoned. They abandoned only their attempt to maintain it by physical force. This principle, on which rest the hopes of the world for spreading and perpetuating free institutions by neighboring State, in my judgment, like the principles of Christianity, ever advances more certainly and safely without resort to arms than with it. ... This principle, therefore, though abandoned in its maintenance on battlefields, still continues to live in all its vigor in the forums of reason, justice, and truth, and will, I trust, continue to live forever. . . . Those who are looking to and desiring ultimate centralism and empire have as yet in their progress that way thus far reached only to the point of attempting to induce by duress certain States as States and as sovereign States to conform to their action under the semblance at least of voluntary consent. — Alexander H. Stephens.
>
>**It is well known that there have always been those among us who wish to enlarge the powers of the general government, and experience would seem to indicate that there is a tendency on the part of this government to overstep the boundaries marked out for it by the Constitution. Its legitimate authority is abundantly sufficient for all the purposes for which it

was created; and its powers being expressly enumerated, there can be no justification for claiming anything beyond them. Every attempt to exercise power beyond these limits should be promptly and firmly opposed. For one evil example will lead to other measures still more mischievous; and if the principles of constructive powers or supposed advantages or temporary circumstances shall ever be permitted to justify the assumption of a power not given by the Constitution, the general government will before long absorb all the powers of legislation, and you will have in effect but one consolidated government. From the extent of our country, its diversified interests, different pursuits, and different habits it is too obvious for argument that a single consolidated government would be wholly inadequate to watch over and protect its interests; and every friend of our free institutions should be always prepared to maintain unimpaired and in full vigor the rights and sovereignty of the States and to confine the action of the general government strictly to the sphere of its appropriate duties. — Andrew Jackson.

In the fourteenth century, when the sturdy sons of Switzerland confronted their Austrian oppressors at Sempach, Arnold Winkelried, commending his family to the care of his countrymen and crying, "Make way for liberty," rushed forward with outstretched hands and, gathering an armful of spears into his own breast, made an opening in the seemingly impenetrable line of the enemy, through which his comrades forced their way to victory. Thus falling in the cause of liberty, he won imperishable fame; and his deed, immortalized in song, has awakened noble and generous emotions and nurtured the love of freedom in the hearts of millions. So shall the story of the men who battled for the Confederacy go down through the ages, kindling the fires of patriotism and devotion to the principles of free government in the hearts of generations to come.

> "Thinking of the mighty dead,
> The young from slothful couch will start,
> And vow with lifted hands outspread,
> Like them to act a noble part."

— Scottish poet, Joanna Baillie (1762-1851)

And so

"... the graves of the dead with the grass overgrown
May yet prove the footstool of liberty's throne,
And each single wreck in the warpath of might
Shall yet be a rock in the temple of right."

— Father Abram Ryan (1839-1866) from the poem "A Land Without Ruins."

A DEFENSE OF THE SOUTH.

IT has been said: "The soldiers of the South needs no apologists or defenders. Their record speaks for them." With reference to their soldierly qualities and achievements, this is indisputably true. Their record shows beyond all question that they were men of splendid courage, patient endurance, and self-sacrificing devotion. Their valiant deeds have won for them a fame which will endure as long as the human heart thrills in response to heroism, and which in years to come, as I believe, will outshine that of the blue-clad legions to whose overwhelming numbers they were at last compelled to yield.

I would not disparage the valor of the Northern soldiers. I saw them make magnificent charges and display admirable courage on many gallantly contested fields. I honor the bravery of the men who so stubbornly resisted the onslaughts of the Confederates in the seven days of fighting around Richmond, who threw themselves with such reckless daring against the almost impregnable position of the Southern troops at Marye's Hill, who fought so fiercely at Chickamauga, and who so gallantly charged up the slopes of Lookout Mountain. They were "foemen worthy of any army's steel." Nevertheless the fact remains that in the conflict between the sections, while the North conquered, the South won the larger measure of glory. As in the estimation of mankind Leonidas and the little band that perished with him at Thermopylae outrank Xerxes and his mighty host, so I believe that in the judgment of coming generations Lee and those who fought under the Starry Cross will rank above Grant and the Grand Army.

They were superb soldiers, those ragged, half-fed, and inadequately equipped men who for four years upheld the battle flag of the South against odds of more than three to one. Even Northern historians have been constrained to admire their superior martial qualities and to use such adjectives as "magnificent" and "incomparable" to describe them. And every paean to the Grand Army of the Republic, every glorification of the two million eight hundred thousand Northern soldiers who were called into service to conquer the South indirectly proclaims the greater glory of the six hundred thousand Southern soldiers whom it took them four years to conquer.

In so far as their soldiership is concerned, it is most certainly true that "the soldiers of the South need no apologists or defenders." Their record places them in the very front rank of the world's soldiery. No men ever fought more bravely, endured hardships more patiently, faced difficulties more resolutely, made sacrifices more cheerfully, or held out longer against such tremendous odds.

But the verdict of the future in regard to the soldiers of the South will be determined not only by their soldierly qualities, but also by the cause in defense of which those qualities were displayed. If it shall be made to appear that they were brave and resolute in upholding an unjust and shameful cause, if posterity shall be led to believe that they were courageous in deliberately and traitorously attacking the life of the nation and willfully plunging the country into the horrors of a fratricidal war to gain selfish and unrighteous ends, their criminality will outweigh their valor in the judgment of the future and they will be deemed infamous rather than inglorious. The luster of glorious achievements on the field of battle is dimmed by time; but the stain of treason, like the "damned spot" on the hand of Lady Macbeth, will not "out."

How many men in this country to-day know anything about the valiant deeds of Benedict Arnold? Not one in a thousand. Yet such deeds were performed by him. It must be admitted that only "an officer of first-rate merit" could have induced even the hardiest veterans to make the long, painful, and difficult march by which he conducted an American force to Quebec; and it is conceded that he behaved with great gallantry in the subsequent assault on that city. Acting as a volunteer, he led the most resolute attack made by the Americans at Saratoga, in which he was badly wounded; and, it is said, to him was largely due the credit for the victory which resulted in the surrender of Burgoyne's army. In soldierly qualities he had few superiors among the Continental officers. Perhaps no braver man ever fought under either the Stars and Stripes or the Starry Cross. But his valiant deeds, obscured by his treason, are no longer remembered with honor, and his name suggests only the blackest infamy.

So, in some measure at least, will it be with the soldiers of the South if the Southern people, by acquiescing in what is said of them by unfriendly historians, permit the crime of causeless rebellion to be fastened upon them. In that case a hundred years hence, when the last Confederate veteran shall have long since gone to join his brave comrades who fell on the field of battle, and his children and most of his grandchildren shall have been numbered with the dead, the splendid courage and heroic achievements of the soldiers of the South will be largely forgotten, and men for the most part will think of them only as rebels and traitors. Hence, while they need no one to defend their record as soldiers, they do need to be defended against misrepresentations of their motives and of the cause for which they fought; they do need to have the false and dishonoring accusations of Northern writers and speakers refuted, so that they may appear before the future with undimmed fame.

And it is not so much a true history as a persistent presentation of the facts given in the histories we have that the South needs. A number of books have been published in which the cause of the South is clearly and faithfully presented and her course fully and unanswerably justified—books eminently fair in their presentation of facts and convincing in their reasoning, which no unprejudiced man can read without being impelled to the conclusion that the Southern soldiers were battling in defense of truth, justice, and freedom. But if the questions discussed in such books are tabooed as "dead issues," and men who dare to speak above a whisper are denounced as foolish and wicked agitators, the books themselves, instead of being read by the people and influencing public opinion, will be left on library shelves to accumulate dust. What the South needs is to have interest in these historic questions kept alive, so that her own people, at least, may be induced to read about them and thus come to have a higher conception of the patriotic motives and a deeper reverence for the self-sacrificing deeds of the statesmen and soldiers of the Southern Confederacy.

The South has ever been too careless of her own fame. She has made history and left the writing of it too much to others. Many of these writers have shown a disposition to diminish rather than magnify her deeds and to withhold from her the praise justly due her. Hence, while her people have ever been foremost in contributing to the common weal and making the country great, by far the larger measure of that greatness is generally placed to the credit of New England, whose people were never backward in recording their own achievements and glorifying themselves. And if their cases were now reversed and New England stood as the South stands to-day, instead of regarding the questions involved in the War between the States as "dead issues" and discouraging all discussion of them as tending to excite bad feeling, she would be flooding the country with literature and would probably have a score of lecturers on the platform setting forth the facts and justifying herself. And something of that sort the South must do if she would not stand before the future with the brand of shame upon her. In the words of a distinguished Southern writer: "If we are willing to be handed down to coming time as a race of slave drivers and traitors, it is as well to continue in our state of lethargy and acquiescence; but if we retain the instincts of men and desire to transmit to our children the untarnished name and spotless fame which our forefathers bequeathed to us, we must awake to the exigencies of the matter."

If the South would not have her children in the years to come wish to forget rather than remember the deeds of their ancestors, instead of permitting the statements of those who are unable to understand her or who willfully misrepresent her to go unquestioned, she must tell her own story and tell it with persistent reiteration. She must refute the charge that her sons, solely to perpetuate slavery, barbarous in its character and condemned by the moral sense of the whole civilized world outside of themselves, renounced their rightful allegiance, rebelled against the government established by the wisdom and patriotism of their fathers, and plunged this country into the horrors of a war in which the lives of hundreds of thousands were sacrificed and almost every home in the land was converted into a house of mourning. This is what she is charged with in most of the so-called histories of the war; and this is what most of her people are acquiescing in, what many of her younger sons and daughters accept as true, and what the outside world generally believes. And yet this charge is false in every particular.

It is not true that slavery as it existed in the South was barbarous. The reports that were formerly circulated in the North of horrible cruelties practiced by Southern slaveholders were mostly pure inventions, malicious lies, deliberately told for the purpose of deceiving the credulous and creating anti-slavery sentiment. Where such reports had the slightest foundation in fact they were gross exaggerations of unusual occurrences.

It is true that there were cruel masters of slaves in the South, just as there are cruel employers of free labor in the North, and just as there always have been and until the millennium dawns always will be cruel men in every business and every quarter of the globe. But these cruel Southern masters were comparatively few, and they were restrained from the practice of cruelty to their slaves by self-interest, by public opinion, and by law. The master who maltreated his slave injured himself by impairing the value of his property, brought on himself the condemnation of his neighbors, and transgressed the humane legal restraints of his power over the slave's person. Naturally such considerations went far to deter even the cruelly disposed from actual cruelty. That slavery as it existed in the South was not cruel and barbarous is evidenced by the almost universal loyalty of the slaves to their masters. As a rule, the Southerner's slaves respected and esteemed him, and were devoted to his interest. In case of danger to his person, they hastened to his rescue. They felt honored by his dignity and shamed by his inferiority, and were eager to uphold his standing in the community. While, much in the same spirit that a child takes jam from the family pantry, they sometimes appropriated to their own use what belonged to him, they permitted no outsider to infringe upon his property rights. They were genuinely interested in all that concerned him—

were proud of his achievements, glad of his successes, sorry for his failures, and moved to sincere sympathy by his bereavements. They honored the mistress of the home, and often denied themselves to please her; befriended and defended the older children of the family, and loved and fondled the younger ones. When the war came and the master, as in thousands of cases, went to the front, leaving his wife and children in their care and at their mercy, their fidelity to the trust thus reposed in them was such as to challenge admiration. Those who are familiar with the facts will readily admit that rarely, if ever, in the history of the world have free laborers given to an employer such affectionate regard and faithful devotion as the Southern slaves gave to their masters. This is utterly inconsistent with the idea that slavery in the South was a cruel and barbarous institution. Had the slaveholders of the South been brutal tyrants, barbarously using their power over those under them, their slaves, by an unfailing law of human nature, instead of regarding them with kindly interest and affection, would have been filled with the spirit of revenge and ready to fly at their throats whenever an opportunity presented itself.

To this day the gray-haired Negro who was a slave and who knows what Southern masters were, will turn to them even though they may be strangers, as the men who understand the Negro best and are his truest friends and surest help in time of need.

The Southern people, it should be remembered, were not responsible for the establishment of slavery among them; they were responsible for its character only. Again and again they protested against the importation of slaves. Their protests were disregarded, and their legislative attempts to prevent it were vetoed by the Crown. They could only make the best of conditions forced upon them. A few years before the war, in a clear and able discussion of slavery in the South, the Hon. Robert Toombs said to a Boston audience:

> The question was not presented for our decision whether it was just or beneficial to the African to tear him away by force or fraud from bondage in his own country and place him in a like condition in ours. England and the Christian world had long before settled that question for us.. At the final overthrow of British authority in these States our ancestors found seven hundred thousand Africans among them, already in bondage and concentrated, from our climate and productions, chiefly in the present slaveholding States. It became their duty to establish governments for themselves and these people, and they brought wisdom, experience, learning, and patriotism to the great work. They sought that system of government which would secure the greatest and most enduring happiness to the whole society. . . . The slaveholding States, . . . finding the African race among them in slavery, unfit to be trusted with political power, incapable as freemen of securing their own happiness or promoting the public prosperity, recognized their condition as slaves and subjected it to legal control." After alluding to the inferiority of the African race as "equally admitted everywhere in the country," Mr. Toombs further said, "The Northern States admit it and, to rid themselves of the burden, inflict the cruelest injuries upon an unhappy race. They expel them from their borders and drive them out of their boundaries as wanderers and outcasts. . . . The Southern States, acting upon the same admitted facts, treat them differently. They keep them in the subordinate condition in which they found them, protect them

against themselves, and compel them to contribute to their own and the public interest and welfare; and under this system we appeal to facts open to all men to prove that the African race has attained a higher degree of comfort and happiness than his race has ever before attained in any other age or country.

The truth is that the slavery which existed in the South, instead of being barbarous in its character, was in accordance with the demands of the most humane civilization and was the wisest and best system that could be devised under the circumstances. It has been well and truthfully said: "Of all rights of man, the right of the ignorant man to be guided by the wiser, to be gently and firmly held in the true course, is the most indispensable. Nature has ordained it from the first. Society has struggled toward perfection by conforming to and accomplishing it more and more. If freedom has any meaning, it means enjoyment of this right, in which all other rights are enjoyed. It is a divine right and duty on both sides and the sum of all social duties between the two." It was in the exercise of this "divine right and duty," so essential to the highest social development, that the Southern people legally subordinated the more ignorant and inferior race placed among them, in spite of their protests, while they were still under the rule of Great Britain. This legal subordination was not based on the assumption that "might makes right," and hence that the white race, having the power, could rightly organize society for its own benefit only; but it was based on the principle that society should be so organized as to bring the greatest possibly good to both races with the least possible injury to either.

That the system of subordination adopted was imperfect, as all human systems are, no one has ever denied; but it was steadily improved as its imperfections became apparent, and, but for ignorant and fanatical intermeddlers, would have been improved still more rapidly. Notwithstanding its imperfections, it brought peace, contentment, and happiness to both races and produced the highest and best social state that ever existed on the American Continent. As Dana maintained in his "Essay on Law as Suited to Man," the domestic relations in which master and servant were recognized and their obligations and duties to each other were well denned, produced "more of mutual good will, more of trust on the one side and fidelity on the other, more of protection and kind care, and more of gratitude and affectionate respect in return, and, because each understood well his place, actually more of a certain freedom, tempered by gentleness and by deference. From the very fact that the distinction of classes was more marked the bond between the individuals constituting these two was closer. As a general truth I verily believe that, with the exception of near-blood relationships and here and there peculiar friendships, the attachment of master and servant was closer and more enduring than that of almost any other connection in life."

That manhood of the highest order was developed under the system of slavery in the South, is attested by almost every page of the country's history; for

Southern men played a leading part in the making of that history. The men of no other section contributed more or even so much to the greatness and glory of the American Republic. No others were braver in battle, wiser in council, more devoted to the common weal, more disinterestedly patriotic, more self-sacrificing in the public service. And whatever may have been the faults of their social and domestic life, they were exceeded by its virtues. They loved pleasure, but they subordinated it to duty. They recognized their responsibilities and faithfully fulfilled their obligations. Their unfailing courtesy and generous hospitality were proverbial. They prized integrity and honor above gain, and disdained injustice, trickery, and meanness. They faced danger with a dauntless spirit and endured adversity with fortitude. A distinguished New England Senator said of them: "They have an aptness for command which makes the Southern gentleman, wherever he goes, not a peer only, but a prince. They have a love for home. They have— the best of them and the most of them— inherited from the great race from which they come, the sense of duty and the instinct of honor as no other people on the face of the earth. . . . They have not the mean traits which grow up somewhere in places where money-making is the chief end of life. They have, above all and giving value to all, that supreme and superb constancy which, without regard to personal ambition and without yielding to the temptation of wealth, without getting tired and without getting diverted, can pursue a great public object in and out, year after year, and generation after generation."

Not only were the "gentlemen" of the South such as Senator Hoar thus described them, but, in the nature of things, their influence acted upon the class beneath them in the social scale, tending to implant in the men of that class a higher "sense of duty" and a keener "instinct of honor." The statement that the slaveholding "aristocrats" looked on labor as dishonoring and depressed the white laborers of the South shows either ignorance of Southern conditions or willful misrepresentation of them. While the planter who owned and directed many slaves, like the employer of many hired men, did not perform manual labor himself, he did not deem such labor dishonoring, and commended the industry of his non-slaveholding neighbors who plowed and sowed and reaped with their own hands. To those poorer neighbors he was always courteous, kind, and helpful. He met them on a friendly footing, felt and showed a sincere interest in their welfare, talked with them in a neighborly way about their difficulties, gave them in unobtrusive advice the benefit of his larger experience and wider knowledge, and in ways that could not offend the most sensitive pride often ministered to their needs. They respected and esteemed him, gathered from him a larger knowledge of men and things, and through association with him gained broader ideas and higher standards of life. The relations which existed between the wealthy slaveholders in the South and those who were unable to own slaves were free from condescension on the one side and envy on the other—friendlier in character and less depressing to the poorer man than those which existed and still exist between the rich and the poor in the North. And under the system of slavery the "poor whites" of the South were, in virtuous womanhood, self-respecting manhood, and all praiseworthy qualities of character and conduct, fully the equals of any similar class in the world.

And this system trained the Negro in habits of industry and order, impressed upon him the idea of obligation and duty, taught him to restrain his appetites and passions and to respect the rights of others, and raised him to a higher level of civilization.

Nor did it subject him to excessive toil. The picture of the heartless slave driver scourging the tired and panting Negro to further exertion is purely imaginary. A Northern writer, telling of what he supposed to be the deplorable conditions existing in the South because of slavery, after looking up statistics, said: "It took five slaves to do the work of one freeman." The freeman must, then, have been driven well-nigh five times as hard as the slave, for in ordinary labor on a farm the negro can accomplish almost as much as the white man. The truth is that, as a rule, the Negro had all his wants supplied, enjoyed many privileges and comforts, and was free from care, contented, and happy. In the days of his strength he worked no more and fared no worse than the boss-driven toilers under the present system; and he had, as they have not, the assurance that when his working days were over he would have an easy seat in the shade by his cabin door in summer, a roof to shelter him and a fire to keep him warm in winter, enough food and clothing and kindly care to make him comfortable until the closing hours of his life, and friendly hands to nurse him tenderly through his last illness, gently close his eyes in death, and reverently lay his body to rest in the grave.

But whether slavery as it existed in the South was humane or barbarous, good or bad, helpful or hurtful to civilization, it is not true that the Southern people withdrew from the Union to perpetuate it. The belief that they did so is not only inconsistent with all their previous history, which is so rich in deeds of devotion to the Union and patriotic sacrifices of their material interests for the common good, but it is altogether incompatible with the conceded intelligence and statesmanship of their leaders. Just a little intelligent consideration of the situation must have convinced them that secession, even if it could be peaceably accomplished, would not in any way establish slavery on a firmer and more enduring basis. They must have seen that secession would not prevent abolitionists from coming South in disguise to steal negroes and incite insurrection; that it would not make the Northern States more willing to enforce the fugitive slave law; that it would not give them any better right or greater power to take their slaves into the Territories, not one foot of which would have been surrendered by the North; and that it would not make slavery any more permanent in the Southern States themselves, where the Federal authorities professed to have neither the right, the power, nor the desire to interfere with it. If they thought about the matter at all, they must have seen that secession, instead of placing slavery on a firmer footing, would make its continued existence more precarious by hopelessly confining it to the States in which it already existed and more fully exposing it to the depredations of slave stealers and the machinations of incendiaries along a border stretching from the Atlantic to the Rio Grande.

By remaining in the Union the South, had she so desired, might have kept slavery in existence for perhaps a quarter of a century longer; for then it could not have been abolished against her will without such a flagrant and tyrannous invasion of her territory and rights as the Northern people would not for years have been prepared to attempt. But had the South been permitted to withdraw from the Union in peace, she could not have maintained slavery for a dozen years. Wendell Phillips saw this, and urged that the Southern States should be permitted to secede peaceably, for, said he, "I believe that dissolution of the Union, sure to result speedily in the abolition of slavery, would be a lesser evil than the slow, faltering disease—the gradual dying out of slavery—constantly poisoning us."

Greg states the case tersely and truly when he says, "To say that the South seceded and fought for slavery is to accuse her of political imbecility." But in the councils of the nation the leaders of the South, the men to whom her people looked for guidance, have ever proved themselves to be at least the peers of the foremost men of the North in logical acumen, political sagacity, and all high qualities of statesmanship. Their worst enemies will not say that they were political imbeciles. Hence they could not have seceded from the Union with the view of thereby perpetuating slavery.

Thousands of Southern men who did not own slaves and thousands of slaveholders who would have sincerely and earnestly favored any wise and just method of emancipation voted for secession, volunteered to serve in the army throughout the war, and bravely fought to uphold the cause of the South. Mr. Stephens expressed the belief that the non-slaveholders of Georgia, while devoted to the Union under the Constitution, were even readier than those who owned slaves to adopt the policy of secession. Surely their aim was not to perpetuate slavery.

But I have heard it said that slavery was the only Southern interest imperiled, that no property right other than that in slaves was in any way threatened, and hence that the protection and perpetuation of slavery must have been the reason for secession. Those who take that view of the matter seem to think that nothing can be dearer to the heart of man than his property. They cannot understand how the men of the South held all mere property rights cheap in comparison with their rights as freemen. They cannot comprehend the Southerner's self-respect, his jealousy of his good name, his quickness to resent insult, his disposition indignantly to spurn any impertinent interference in his affairs, his spirit of independence, his unwavering devotion to self-government, and his readiness at all times to imperil fortune and life in defense of his honor or his principles. These characteristics, roused to activity by the attacks of Northern writers and speakers and by the danger to self-government involved in the avowed Northern policy in regard to slavery, fully account for the secession of the Southern States from the Union.

For many years the anti-slavery party at the North had actively pursued the policy of attacking the South in the most libelous and exasperating manner. Emissaries in various guises, from peddlers to preachers, were sent into the Southern States "to spy out the land" and to take advantage of any opportunity to further the aims of the abolitionists, whether by opening the eyes of the Southern master to the enormity of his wickedness and inducing him to don the robe of Northern righteousness, or by inciting his slaves to rise up against him and "cut his throat." The country was flooded with writings of the most defamatory character, telling of imaginary cruelties and barbarities practiced on the slaves of the South and denouncing Southerners as "brutal tyrants, man-stealers, and murderers." Says Mr. Lunt in his "Origin of the Late War:"

> The plague became at length in its degree like that of the swarms of frogs and flies and locusts. Indeed, in the wild conception of the more fervid devotees of emancipation the 'Sunny South' was likened to the land of Egypt, in which the children of Ham were blasphemously symbolized as the chosen people of the Almighty; and the new, self-delegated prophets who were to work out their deliverance, with neither visible sign nor accredited mission, were these presumptuous Northern agitators and pamphleteers.

Some idea of the spirit of hate that animated these "self-delegated prophets" and led them utterly to disregard truth, justice, and law to accomplish their ends may be gathered from the following: "It is our honest conviction that all the proslavery slaveholders deserve at once to be reduced to a parallel with the basest criminals that lie fettered within the cells of our public prisons. . . . Our banner is inscribed: 'No cooperation with slaveholders in politics; no fellowship with them in religion; no affiliation with them in society; no recognition of proslavery men except as ruffians, outlaws, and criminals.' . . . We are determined to abolish slavery at all hazards, in defiance of all the opposition, of whatever nature, it is possible for the slaveocrats to bring against us." (As the "slaveocrats" had never opposed them and did not intend to oppose them, except with the Constitution, this last declaration was a distinct avowal of the determination to accomplish their purpose in defiance of the provisions of that instrument.) The book of which the foregoing extracts are samples received the written commendation of more than sixty Republican members of Congress and of many of the most prominent Republicans out of Congress. It was specially recommended for circulation as a campaign document. Of it Mr. William H. Seward said, "It seems to me a work of great merit, . . . and I do not doubt it will exert a great influence on the public mind in favor of truth and justice."

Another emanation from the Northern press was a pamphlet, said to have been widely circulated in both the North and the South, declaring the purpose "to land military forces" and "raise the standard of freedom" in the Southern States—a purpose which

John Brown attempted to carry out. The pamphlet said:

> Our plan is to make war openly or secretly, as circumstances may dictate, upon the property of the slaveholders and their abettors, not for its destruction, if that can be easily avoided, but to convert it to the use of the slaves. If it cannot be thus converted, we advise its destruction. Teach the slaves to burn their masters' buildings, to kill their cattle and hogs, to conceal and destroy farming utensils, to abandon labor in seedtime and harvest and let the crops perish.

This is a specimen of the much-boasted Northern philanthropy and superior brand of morality.

For a quarter of a century before the war the South was the object of such slanderous and incendiary attacks, issuing from pulpit and press; and naturally they produced in the Southern people the deepest indignation and a burning sense of wrong. The people of the South resented Northern interference with slavery in any way as an insult to them and an impudent obtrusion. They claimed that slavery as it existed among them was exclusively their business, to be managed by them as they thought best. It was not attachment to slavery, but indignation excited by the infamous slanders and contemptible methods of Northern meddlers with it that impelled them to action. Mr. Toombs truly said in the United States Senate, "Well, sir, the question of slavery moves not the people of Georgia one-half as much as the fact that you insult their rights as a community. You abolitionists are right when you say that there are thousands and tens of thousands of men in Georgia and all over the South who do not own slaves. A very large portion of the people of Georgia own none of them. In the mountains there are comparatively few of them, but no part of our people are more loyal to their race and country than our bold and brave mountain population. . . . They say, and well say, 'This is our question. . . . We will tell you when we choose to abolish this thing. It must be done under our direction and according to our will. Our own, our native land shall determine this question, and not the abolitionists of the North.' That is the spirit of our freemen." And that spirit actuated the people throughout the South. It was not the determination to uphold and perpetuate slavery, but the determination to resent the insulting interference and spurn the insolent dictation of the North.

Southern statesmen—those to whom the people of the South looked for advice and guidance, and who were really responsible for secession—shared, of course, in this general feeling of indignation; but they were actuated by still higher considerations. Beneath the agitation of the slavery question they saw, as all the world may now see, a deliberate attack upon the principle of confederation on which the Union was formed, and which they held to be essential to the preservation of the liberties of the people. They clearly perceived, as Mr. Jefferson perceived in 1820, that Northern Federalists or, more properly, Centralists, were taking advantage of the sentiment against slavery to get control of the government and enlarge its powers. They were thoroughly convinced that, as Mr. Stephens says, "It was the object of the Centralists, by using this question, to accomplish their purpose of effecting a consolidated empire instead of continuing the Federal republic." They firmly believed that, however honest and conscientious the great majority of the antislavery party might be, the men who were directing that party had designs above and beyond any action tending to bring about the emancipation of slaves, and that their purpose was to establish a national government clothed with sovereign power over the States instead of a federal government acting as the common agent of sovereign States and having no powers except those delegated to it in the compact of union.

The whole history of the Congressional controversy in regard to slavery indicated such a design on the part of the leaders of the antislavery party. It is a fact commonly overlooked yet highly significant that in all the debates in Congress relating to the subject the real question was not as to the right or wrong of slavery, not as to whether it ought or ought not be restricted or abolished, but as to whether Congress was authorized to decide the matter. Long and bitter as the controversy was, it was not a conflict between those who favored and those who opposed slavery, but a conflict between those who favored and those who opposed the usurpation of power by the Federal authorities; and if many patriotic antislavery men from the Northern States had not voted against it, such usurpation would have been an accomplished fact long before 1861.

A petition asking the Federal authorities to deal with the subject of slavery was presented to Congress as early as 1700. Some members of that body were opposed to entertaining it on the ground that Congress had nothing to do with the matter, but the majority deemed it best to consider it and to state plainly that the subject was one concerning which Congress had no authority to act. A resolution to that effect was adopted, a majority of the members from the Northern States, some of whom had been prominent in the Convention that framed the Constitution, voting for it. The resolution said nothing as to the right or wrong of slavery, but merely declared "That Congress have no authority to interfere in the emancipation of slaves or in the treatment of them within any of the States, it remaining with the several States alone to provide any regulations therein which humanity and true policy may require." The only question involved in this early consideration of the subject by Congress was the authority of that body to legislate in regard to it. And the censure of Southern men in later years for alleged opposition to the right of petition was all based on the fact that they opposed the consideration and discussion of petitions to do what they had no authority to do. They regarded the consideration and discussion of such petitions as not only useless, but harmful.

In the debates on the admission of Missouri to Statehood, when the subject of slavery first assumed a decidedly threatening aspect, the same question of Congressional authority was the only real issue. When the bill for the admission of Missouri into the Union as a State was presented in the usual way, an amendment was offered prohibiting the further introduction of slavery except for the punishment of crimes, and providing that all children born within the State after its admission into the Union should be free at the age of twenty-five years. Congressmen, from the North and from the South alike, aligned themselves for or against this amendment not according to their views of the propriety of restricting slavery, but according to their views of the authority of Congress to restrict it. Men who were thoroughly antislavery in sentiment strongly opposed the amendment on the ground that Congress could not lawfully impose such a restriction on the people of Missouri and thus deprive them of the right to determine for themselves the character of their domestic institutions. They held that such action by Congress would involve the assumption of power not given to that body by the Constitution. Among those who held this view was the eloquent and patriotic John Holmes, of Massachusetts. He saw in the move an attempt to resuscitate the Federalist or centralizing party of New England, and after crediting most of its supporters with honesty, he said: "But is it not probable that there are some jugglers behind the screen who are playing a deeper game, who are combining to rally under this standard as a last resort, the forlorn hope of an expiring party? . . . For one, sir, I would rejoice if there was not a slave on earth. Liberty is the object of my love, my adoration. I would extend its blessings to every human being. But though my feelings are strong for the abolition of slavery, they are yet stronger for the Constitution of my country. And if I am reduced to the sad alternative, to tolerate the holding of slaves in

Missouri or violate the Constitution of my country, I will not admit a doubt to cloud my choice."

And so in all the debates about slavery in the Territories, extending down to the commencement of the war and often exceedingly bitter, the only pertinent question was that as to Federal jurisdiction— that as to the authority of Congress to legislate on the subject. And while many Northern men, like Mr. Holmes, were patriotic enough to stand firmly with the representatives of the South in opposition to any legislation not authorized by the Constitution, the leaders of the antislavery party, from first to last, insisted on such legislation.

Not only by persistently urging that Congress should exercise legislative authority not granted by the Constitution, but by their speeches in and out of Congress and by their general policy these leaders plainly indicated a purpose to disregard the limitations of the Constitution and enlarge the Federal powers. Notwithstanding all their professions of love for the negro, the course pursued by them showed that they were politicians rather than philanthropists; that they aimed, in subversion of the Constitution, to establish a strong government, controlled by themselves or their section; and that, instead of endeavoring to devise some just, reasonable, practicable, and amicable plan of settling the slavery question, they desired to keep up a constant agitation of the subject as a means of accomplishing their ambitious designs.

The purpose thus indicated by the leaders of the antislavery party in Congress was still more clearly manifested by the action of that party throughout the country. In the Chicago Convention it rejected the word "national" as descriptive of its character and placed itself on a distinctly sectional basis. It thus substituted sectional animosity for the spirit of fraternity and mutual assistance which brought the States into alliance, politically dissolved the Union, and virtually declared war against the South. The author of "The Origin of the Late War" very truly says,

> It is impossible to regard the proceedings of the Chicago Convention in any other light than as equivalent to a proclamation of absolutely hostile purposes against the Southern section of the country. They were not technically a declaration of war, to be conducted by arms, simply because they professed only to use the pacific force of superior numbers in order to deprive the minority of its rights under the Constitution. While in one part of their platform the Republicans made a specious profession of regard for the Constitution, in another part they announced a dissolution of the 'political bands' by which the sections were held together and even refused to be called by a national name. It was an attitude which ought to have given instant alarm to every sincere friend of the Union.

To effect their hostile purposes against the South the Republicans found it necessary to refuse to fulfill their obligations under the Constitution and to nullify Federal laws enacted to make its provisions more effective. To justify this they enunciated the doctrine of a "higher law"—a law which, as it was illustrated by the conduct of those who professed to be guided by it, made all obligations and restraints imposed by the government subordinate to their ideas, aims, and wishes.

In obedience to this so-called "higher law," the act of Congress intended to make the constitutional provision for the rendition of fugitive slaves more effective was flagrantly and boastfully set at naught. Mass meetings were held throughout the North to create and intensify opposition to its enforcement, popular assemblies adopted resolutions in regard to it (which Mr. Webster declared to be tantamount to "levying war against the government"), and the legislative bodies of a majority of the Northern States enacted laws which practically nullified it. The most noted writers and speakers of the Republican Party openly avowed their determination to deal with the subject of slavery not according to the provisions of the Constitution, but according to their own notion of what ought to be done.

Mr. Garrison, the chief among the ultra-abolitionists, unable to deny the fact that the Constitution recognized the claims of the South as just, declared that instrument to be "a covenant with death and an agreement with hell."

The Rev. Henry Ward Beecher, the ablest among the many clergymen who preached the gospel of a "higher law," who probably knew more about theology than he did about the principles of government, overlooking the fact that the Constitution was the foundation of the Union and that without the foundation the superstructure could not stand, attempted to refute the idea that the preservation of the former was necessary to the preservation of the latter by denying the identity of the two, declaring "the Constitution itself" to be "the cause of every division" occasioned by "the vexed question of slavery," and thus inferentially teaching that the country could get rid of the whole trouble by getting rid of the Constitution.

The Hon. William H. Seward, the most influential politician and the acknowledged leader of the party, who would almost certainly have been its candidate for the presidency had it not been deemed expedient to bid for Western votes by nominating a man from that section, fully exemplified the "higher law" doctrine which he enunciated. Of him and his disciples an eminent jurist said, "In words perfectly free from ambiguity and by a long series of public acts which admit of no doubtful construction, Mr. Seward taught disobedience to the Constitution as a duty and contempt for it as a patriotic sentiment. This principle (if it be lawful to call it a principle) was adopted, avowed, and acted upon by his party with almost entire unanimity whenever and wherever they found their wishes opposed by a constitutional interdict. By him and by them the old notion that the law of the land ought to be obeyed was scoffed at."

According to the testimony of Mr. Seward, the party's candidate for the presidency was fully committed to the "higher law" policy and intended, if elected, to make it the policy of his administration. In a speech delivered in Boston Mr. Seward said: "The people have for their standard bearer Abraham Lincoln, confessing the obligations of the 'higher law' . . . and contending for weal or woe, for life or death in the irrepressible conflict between freedom and slavery. I desire only to say that we are in the last stage of the conflict, before the great triumphant inauguration of this policy into the government of the United States."

In brief, the Republican party, with all its fanatical reformers, meddlesome preachers, and ambitious politicians, repudiated the Constitution and proposed to set up in its stead a so-called "higher law," under which those in power might exceed all constitutional limitations and administer the government according to their own judgment or interest, a "higher law" of which one of the ablest jurists in the country said: "It is simply not law at all, but license to use political power in any way that will promote the interests or gratify the passions of him who wields it. It tells those who administer the government that they may do whatever they can do. It abolishes all law and puts in its place the mere force which law was made to control."

This presented the real issue in the conflict between the sections. It was not a conflict between the antislavery party and a proslavery party, for there never was a proslavery party—a party organized to uphold slavery—in American politics. The party which has been so designated had in its ranks many who were opposed to slavery, and was in reality the pro-Constitution party—the party which at all times earnestly protested against the assumption by the Federal authorities of powers not conferred on them by the Constitution.

The men of this party were as much opposed to unconstitutional action by the Federal government in favor of slavery as they were to such action against slavery. For example, when Mr. Green, of Missouri, offered a resolution in the Senate suggesting the propriety of a "law for establishing an armed police force at all necessary points along the line separating the slaveholding States from the non-slaveholding States, for the purpose of maintaining the general peace between those States, of preventing the invasion of one State by the citizens of another, and also for the more efficient execution of the fugitive slave laws," Mr. Davis, of Mississippi, said: "I do not comprehend the policy of a Southern Senator who would seek to change the whole form of our government and substitute Federal force for State obligation and authority. Do we want a new government that is to overthrow the old? Do we wish to erect a central colossus, wielding at discretion the military arm and exercising military force over the people of the States?" And, on the supposition that Mr. Green's resolution meant to give the Federal government a power, not already possessed by it, to compel States to fulfill their constitutional obligation to surrender fugitive slaves, Mr. Davis further said: "He is providing, under the name of Union, to carry on a war against States; and, I care not whether it be against Massachusetts or Missouri, it is equally objectionable to me, and I will resist it alike in the one case and in the other as subversive of the great principle on which our government rests, as a heresy to be confronted at its first presentation and put down there lest it grow into proportions which will render us powerless before it."

This was the position of all the leading men of the South. They were immovably opposed to any assumption of extra-constitutional powers by the Federal government, as tending to deprive the States of their sovereignty and to establish what Mr. Lincoln in the Hampton Roads Conference called "national authority," and what he said the Southern States must recognize before he would consent to even a suspension of hostilities for the purpose of considering terms of peace. Southern men clung most tenaciously to the rights of the States—to the independence of each of the original thirteen as having been won from Great Britain and never surrendered, and to the independence of each of the others as having been admitted into the Union on an equal footing with them. They held the maintenance of State independence to be essential to the preservation of their liberties, and in comparison with this they regarded the subject of slavery as but a "drop in the ocean." As Mr. Stephens said: "Even the two thousand million dollars invested in the relation thus established, between private capital and the labor of this class of population, under the system, was but as the dust in the balance compared with the vital attributes of the rights of independence and sovereignty on the part of the several States."

Thus valuing the rights of the several States, the representative men of the South and many wise and patriotic men of the North were unalterably opposed to the "higher law" policy or any other policy that would authorize the Federal government to exceed in any way whatever the powers delegated to it by the Constitution. They urged strict obedience to the Constitution as "the supreme law to every American," the "plighted faith of our fathers," and the "hope of posterity." They saw that if the provisions of the Constitution in regard to slavery could be disregarded on the ground of morality, expediency, necessity, or any other so-called "higher law," its provisions in regard to other things could with equal right be violated on the same ground; that all constitutional guarantees and safeguards would thus be rendered worthless; and that, instead of a government administered according to the organic law of the Union, we might thus come to have a government administered according to what any party in power might deem expedient and right, and therefore a "higher law." Hence they insisted that the provisions of the Constitution in regard to slavery and every other question should be held inviolate.

However it may have been overshadowed and obscured by giving prominence to subordinate matters, this was the real issue. The claim of the South was unreserved obedience to the Constitution. Wherein it may be found inadequate, amend it in the prescribed way; but until it is thus amended, its provisions must be fully carried out. The claim of the North was "There is a law higher than the Constitution," and wherein the Constitution conflicts with that higher law it must be disobeyed. The South was dominated by the principle of "Law and Order"— the principle of conformity to the lawfully established order and the remedy of wrongs in a lawful way. The North was dominated by what Wendell Phillips called "The Puritan Principle"— the principle of those whose motto, as Mr. Phillips declared, was not "Law and Order," but "God and Justice," and who were always ready to tread down law and order in the effort to compel others to conform to their notion of God and justice. The South was ever loyal to the compact of union, and in all respects faithfully fulfilled the obligations it imposed; the North was disloyal to that compact, and flagrantly violated its terms. Hence if the War Between the States may be rightly called "The War of the Rebellion," the rebels lived north of the Potomac.

In "The Origin of the Late War" Mr. Lunt, a Northern man, says: "Without meaning to institute any disparaging comparison, it may be remarked with justice that the middle class of men at the South, whether owing to larger leisure or to whatever cause, have in general more closely attended to and more clearly understood the principles of our government than the same class at the North." And the same author, after stating that "there were here and there zealous dis-unionists in the South, as there were at the North," says: "But it cannot be doubted that during the progress of these events the vast body of the people in every slave State, including the most able, influential, and by far the most in number of their leading men, were heartily attached to the Union, sincerely anxious to preserve it, and desired only to maintain unimpaired in their original purity and integrity those principles of the Constitution, whether right or wrong in some of their interpretations of them, upon which the Union was founded and which were essential to its preservation."

The leading men of the South were so devoted to the Union and so reluctant to withdraw from it that, even after the triumph of the distinctly sectional party at the polls and the election of a President avowedly hostile to Southern institutions and interests, they would not have seceded if they could have obtained any satisfactory assurance that the Constitution would continue to be recognized as the law of the land and that the government would continue to be administered in accordance with its plain provisions. This assurance they vainly tried to get. The testimony of Judge Black, of Pennsylvania, given in an open letter to the Hon. Charles Francis Adams, which was published in the Galaxy for January 1874, not only confirms this statement, but throws a flood of light on the whole situation. After stating the general belief at Washington that Mr. Seward would be "the Wolsey of the new administration, with "Law in his voice and honor in his hand,' while others would be subordinate and the President himself little more than a figurehead," Judge Black said: "When the troubles were at their worst certain Southern gentlemen, through Judge Campbell, of the Supreme Court, requested me to meet Mr. Seward and see if he would not give them some ground on which they could stand with safety inside of the Union. I consented, and we met at the State Department. . . . Many propositions were discussed and rejected as being either impracticable or likely to prove useless before I told him what I felt perfectly sure would stop all controversy at once and forever. I proposed that he should simply pledge himself and the incoming administration to govern according to the Constitution, and upon every disputed point of constitutional law to accept that exposition of it which had been or might be given by the judicial authorities. He started at this, became excited, and violently declared he would do no such thing. 'That, said he, 'is treason; that would make me agree to the Dred Scott case.' In vain I told him that he was not required to admit the correctness of any particular case, but merely to submit to it [the Constitution] as the decision of the highest tribunal, from which there could be no appeal except to the sword. I had never before heard that treason was obedience to the Constitution as construed by the courts; but this prepared me to learn, as I did some time afterwards, that the correlative virtue of loyalty consisted in trampling the laws underfoot."

Thus the recognized leader of the Republican party, who was expected to dictate the policy of the incoming administration, emphatically refused to give the Southern leaders that assurance of safety within the Union which would have settled all the trouble, and declared that it would be treason to pledge himself and his party to govern according to the Constitution as it had been or might be expounded by the highest judicial tribunal in the country.

When the reins of government were placed in the hands of men who thus emphatically refused to pledge themselves to govern according to the Constitution as construed by the judiciary; when the administration of the country's affairs was given to a party that was organized on a distinctly sectional basis and, in the words of a Northern historian, "Constitution and Union and all public and personal rights and privileges dependent upon them, in the North as well as in the South, stood in immediate and imminent danger of utter overthrow," Southern statesmen felt that, if they would preserve the government inherited from their fathers and hand it down as a heritage to their children, they must withdraw from the Union and establish a Confederacy of their own. They were moved by no feeling of disloyalty. The South had always been loyal to the government. Her sons had been most prominent in its formation and most conspicuous in promoting its success and glory. That they were still loyal to it is evidenced by the fact that they made it their own. They framed no new Constitution, organized no new form of government, but adopted the old Constitution as the fundamental law of their new Confederacy, making only a few changes in the wording to guard against any possible misconstruction, and a few additional provisions looking to the remedy of evils not foreseen by its framers—provisions which the New York Herald at the time declared to be "invaluable reforms" that "should be adopted by the United States with or without the return of the seceded States, and as soon as possible." As President of the Southern Confederacy and using the words in precisely the same sense, Mr. Davis might have repeated the following statement made by him in the Senate of the

United States: "Our flag bears no new device. Upon its folds our principles are written in living light, all proclaiming the constitutional union, justice, equality, and fraternity of our domain." In his inaugural address he did say, "The Constitution founded by our fathers is that of these Confederate States in their exposition of it." And their exposition of it was that of the Convention which framed it; of all the States that originally sanctioned it and confederated under it; of three-fourths of the States, voting through their representatives in the Senate, in 1838; of nearly two-thirds of the States, voting in the same way, in the spring of 1860; of the ablest jurists in the country, both North and South; and of the highest judicial tribunal in the United States.

Not in the spirit of rebellion against the government established by the fathers of the republic, but in the spirit of loyalty to that government, the people of the South refused to acquiesce in its subversion and formed a new Confederacy to perpetuate it unimpaired.

They earnestly desired to withdraw from the Union peaceably, and did everything consistent with their safety and honor to avert the horrors of war. They hoped that, notwithstanding the false and subversive teaching of the Republican party, the great body of the Northern people still held the doctrine, enunciated in the Declaration of Independence, that "Governments derive their just powers from the consent of the governed," and that, holding this doctrine, they would not attempt to govern the South without her consent. And this hope might have been realized but for the fact that President Lincoln, instead of submitting the question to the representatives of the people in Congress, who alone had the constitutional right to make war, usurped the war-making power and began hostile measures.

When war was forced upon them, the people of the South proved themselves to be brave and worthy defenders of the right of self-government which their fathers had won from Great Britain and bequeathed to them as a priceless heritage. For four years they upheld that right against an enemy greatly outnumbering them and having incalculably larger resources, better equipments, and more effective means of waging war. They displayed courage, devotion, and heroism never surpassed and rarely equaled in the history of the world. Their deeds of valor challenged universal admiration, and, told in song and story, they will excite feelings of wonder and praise in the hearts of men through the ages to come.

But notwithstanding the justice of her cause and the valor of her sons, the South failed. When she had become a land of graves in which were sleeping many thousands of her bravest and best, when the ranks of her armies were so depleted that she could not muster men enough to form a thin line of battle along the enemy's extended and doubly manned front, when her resources were so exhausted that she could no longer give sufficient food and clothing to the remnant of her brave defenders, when her powers of resistance were so weakened that to prolong the struggle would be but a useless and criminal sacrifice of life, she lowered her flag in surrender, and another chapter was added to the history of successful usurpations and the triumphs of might over right.

> "Yet raise thy head, fair land!
> Thy dead died bravely for the right;
> The folded flag is stainless still,
> The broken sword is bright;
> No blot is on thy record found;
> No treason soils thy fame."

NOTE: The above lines are from "THE NINTH of APRIL, 1865, a poem by English historian, Percy Greg.

And when thy history is impartially and fairly written, disclosing the pure and patriotic motives and recounting the heroic deeds of thy sons, it will "bear

> This blazon to the last of times;
> No nation rose so white and fair
> Or fell so pure of crimes."

The above lines are from the inscription on the Confederate monument in Augusta, Georgia, which was unveiled on October 31, 1878. — Ed.

CAVALIER LOYALTY AND PURITAN DISLOYALTY IN AMERICA.

APPOMATTOX was a triumph of the physically stronger in a conflict between the representatives of two essentially different civilizations and antagonistic ideas of government. On one side in that conflict was the South, led by the descendants of the Cavaliers, who, with all their faults, had inherited from a long line of ancestors a manly contempt for moral littleness, a high sense of honor, a lofty regard for plighted faith, a strong tendency to conservatism, a profound respect for law and order, and an unfaltering loyalty to constitutional government. Against the South was arrayed the power of the North, dominated by the spirit of Puritanism, which, with all its virtues, has ever been characterized by the Pharisaism that worships itself and is unable to perceive any goodness apart from itself; which has ever arrogantly held its ideas, its interests, and its will to be higher than fundamental law and covenanted obligations; which has always "lived and moved and had its being" in rebellion against constituted authority; which, with the cry of freedom on its lips, has been one of the most cruel and pitiless tyrants that ever cursed the world; which, while beheading an English king in the name of liberty, brought England under a reign of oppression whose little finger was heavier than the mailed hand of the Stuarts; and which, from the time of Oliver Cromwell to the time of Abraham Lincoln, has never hesitated to trample upon the rights of others in order to effect its own ends.

The preceding paragraph, taken from a speech which I delivered in Richmond, Virginia, was bitterly assailed by some of the Northern papers. Notwithstanding the fact that "the grim and strenuous Puritan spirits of New England" have been celebrated in song and story; notwithstanding the fact that succeeding generations have hallowed their memory and highly extolled their work as "crusaders of liberty;" notwithstanding the fact, or what I supposed to be the fact, that to prove one's descent from an ancestor who "came over on the Mayflower" was to go far toward making his "title clear" to be received into the most exclusive New England society—notwithstanding all this, many Northern editors seemed to think it an insult to the Northern people to intimate that they were in any way connected with or influenced by Puritanism.

One editor, blinded by his resentment, I suppose, failed to see what just a little attention to the context would have shown him—that my reference was to political rather than religious Puritanism—and endeavored to even matters by asserting that the Northern people had departed from the faith and practice of the early Puritans, and that at the time of the war the South was more puritanically religious than the North. Another fancied that in what I said there was an absurd claim of Cavalier descent for all Southerners and Puritan descent for all Northerners, and proceeded to overthrow this imaginary claim by saying, "If there had been no Southern soldiers except descendants of Cavaliers and no Northern soldiers except descendants of Cromwellian Puritans, the Civil War could have been fought under a circus tent." Another, with wonderful acumen, discovered in what I said a dividing line "separating the sections into areas of virtue and vice" and putting all the virtue down South and all the vice up North. Yet another found in my language a "denunciation of Northern men as sordid oppressors and malignant hypocrites."

Had those who thus criticised this paragraph taken time to consider calmly its meaning instead of permitting themselves to be carried away by anger, I think they would have found in it nothing to excite their-wrath or justify their criticisms. Fairly interpreted, it does not reflect on or in any way refer to the religion of either section. Neither does it disparage the ancestry of the people of either section. It does not deny, either directly or indirectly, the well-known fact that there were men of Cavalier descent in the North and men of Puritan descent in the South, and that probably a majority of the people of both sections were descended from neither Cavaliers nor Puritans. There is in it nothing fairly suggestive of the idea that the country is or ever was "separated into areas of virtue and vice"— nothing inconsistent with the fact that in each section there are good and bad, that each has its virtues and each has its vices, that in each there is much to commend and much to condemn, and that neither can justly claim to be morally superior to the other. The charge that it "denounces Northern men as sordid oppressors and malignant hypocrites" is altogether groundless. It neither praises nor censures the men of the North—contains no allusion to their moral qualities as good or bad. Its language refers not to Northern men, but to the spirit of Puritanism—the ruling temper, disposition, or principle which is exhibited in the history of the Puritans, and which, represented by a few radical leaders, got control of affairs in the North in 1860. Even that spirit is not characterized as "sordid" and "hypocritical."

In this whole statement there is not one word about the merits or demerits of either the Northern or the Southern people. The statement merely contrasts the two spirits or principles which became pronounced and dominated the two sections just before the war: the Cavalier spirit, characterized by a fidelity to its sense of honor and a contempt for indirect methods that led it to keep plighted faith, to be loyal to constituted government, and to assert its rights openly and boldly; and the Puritan spirit—characterized by an absolute confidence in the truth and righteousness of its own ideas and policies and a determination to enforce those ideas and policies at whatever cost—that blinded it to the good in anything that opposed it, caused it to rebel against constituted authority, and led it sternly and uncompromisingly to pursue its ends regardless of the rights of others. Some may name those two spirits Conservatism and Progress—the disposition blindly and stubbornly to adhere to the old order and the disposition to change the old order so as to bring it into accord with increased enlightenment and higher ideas. But however they may be named, there they were, in 1860, confronting each other: the one a heritage from the Cavalier and the other a heritage from the Puritan; the one dominating the South and the other dominating the North. And the conflict between them brought on the war.

The essential point in the contrast drawn between these two spirits is that one is the spirit of obedience to "the powers that be" and the other is the spirit of disobedience to "the powers that be" if those powers require what it does not approve. The one is the spirit of loyalty to constituted government; the other is the spirit of disloyalty to constituted government wherein that government does not conform to its ideas. The one subordinates itself to the law; the other sets itself above the law. This difference between them is so clearly marked in history that it must be apparent even to one who reads with half-opened eyes.

I have forgotten who said,[1] "My country! May she always be right! But, right or wrong, my country;" but with the substitution of "king" for "country," his words exactly express the sentiment of the courageous and faithful hearts who rallied around the royal standard in England's great civil war. It is a false sentiment—a sentiment which has led many brave men to battle on the side of wrong. But it was the sentiment of the English Cavaliers. Doubtless many of them, like the accomplished and liberal-minded

---

[1] Stephen Decatur (1779-1829) was one of the fathers of the United States Navy. He is credited with the above quote by most historians. — *Ed.*

Falkland, disapproved the king's acts and distrusted him; but, like the chivalrous Sir Edmund Verney, they would "not do so base a thing as to desert him." They bared their swords in his defense with a devotion that was illustrated by the Marquis of Winchester, who, when his house, which he "had held stoutly out through the war for the king," was finally taken by storm, and he stood, a prisoner, viewing the flames that were reducing it to a shapeless pile of ruins, said that, "If the king had no more ground in England but Basing House, he would adventure it as he did and so maintain it to the uttermost;" for "Basing House was called 'loyalty.'"

These men were not fighting for Charles the man, but for Charles the king. And they were not fighting for the king in the spirit of base submission. They did not take up arms in obedience to his call because they dared not assert their rights against him. They defended him because he stood to them for the established order, which both the preservation of their honor and the maintenance of their rights required them to uphold. He was the rightful heir to the throne, the ruler to whom they owed allegiance; and they felt that it would be dishonorable to turn against him or refuse to draw their swords in his defense. With all his faults, he was to them the lawful representative of the English monarchy, with all of glory and of good that centuries of struggle and growth had gathered about it. He may have abused his power, as many of his predecessors on the throne had done, but he was to them still the legitimate head of the English government, whom they must defend in order to preserve that government.

Macaulay, while frankly declaring his belief that "the cause of the king was the cause of bigotry and tyranny," "cannot refrain from looking with complacency on the character of the honest old Cavaliers" who fought in defense of it. After pointing out the unfairness of charging upon them the profligacy and baseness of the lawless crew who were attracted to the standard of Charles by the hope of license and plunder, he says: "Our royalist countrymen were not heartless, dangling courtiers, bowing at every step and simpering at every word. It was not for a treacherous king or an intolerant Church that they fought, but for the old banner which had waved in so many battles over the heads of their fathers, and for the altars at which they had received the hands of their brides."

A goodly number of men thus loyal to that "old banner" and those "altars" had come to America before the outbreak of the war between king and Parliament; and when that war ended so disastrously for the royalists, many crossed the Atlantic to find a refuge from the pitiless vengeance of the victorious party. Naturally they did not go to New England, where the people had no sympathy with them, but landed on the shores of Virginia, where Governor Berkeley, a stanch adherent of monarchy, was ready to receive them "with open arms and purse," and the planters would entertain them with lavish hospitality and give them liberal aid. In the month of September 1649, one ship brought to Virginia more than three hundred of these refugees, and all through the years of the Commonwealth the tide of Cavalier immigration continued.

These royalist exiles were, for the most part, men of some prominence, for had they been obscure adherents of the king, they could have remained in England with safety. Among them were many "men of the first rate," who wanted not money nor credit, and had fled from their native country as from a place infected with the plague." They and their descendants became the "landed gentry" from whom, "with but a slight infusion of yeomanry," says Doyle, the colony "drew its governing class." They became the leaders of Virginia, molding the opinions of her people, giving character to her society, directing her affairs, and shaping her policies. As Cooke maintains, "the mass of the Virginia population and a vast preponderance of the wealth and influence of the colony were Cavalier—always taking the word to mean friendly to Church and king."

And, naturally, the temper, teaching, and example of these stanch royalists were not without influence on the thoughts and sentiments of their children. If, as we are told, the prominent characteristics of men are transmitted to their progeny, and, though modified by changed conditions, are ineradicable, surely the unfaltering loyalty which characterized the men who freely staked their fortunes and lives in defense of the English monarchy must, in some measure at least, have been transmitted to many generations of their descendants.

That the sentiment of loyalty was deeply rooted in the hearts of the Virginians in subsequent years is clearly evident from the facts bearing on the question. If loyalty does not mean the obedience of abject slaves who are afraid to urge a reasonable objection to burdens unlawfully laid upon them, if it be not disloyal to remonstrate firmly but respectfully against the infringement of chartered rights and solicit the redress of grievances, nothing done by the men of Virginia during the entire colonial period can be rightly termed disloyal. They faithfully performed their duties as citizens and fully discharged every obligation involved in allegiance to the crown. When an unworthy representative of the king, like the "extortionate, unjust, and arbitrary" Governor Harvey, "multiplied penalties and exactments and appropriated fines to his own use," they "thrust him out of his government" and appointed another in his stead. But this action, instead of being rebellion against the king, was made subject to the king's pleasure; and when the king decided against them, they took back the unjust governor. If any reigning monarch, probably misinformed and misled by his advisers, attempted to deprive them of rights and privileges previously granted to them, they resisted with memorial setting forth the facts and respectfully protesting against the attempt; but they resorted to no violent or unlawful methods of resistance. They never surrendered their rights, but they maintained those rights in the spirit of loyalty and by means wholly consistent with their allegiance.

Bacon's Rebellion, which some have represented as "armed defiance of England," was, on the part of Bacon's followers at least, no intentional defiance of England in any way. In the beginning it was nothing more than an expedition against the Indians, unauthorized by the governor and in opposition to his wishes. When the governor denounced those who took part in the expedition as rebels, it became a fight between him and them, in which the people naturally sympathized with their resolute defenders against the savages. Whatever may have been in the mind of Bacon himself, it is evident that few, if any, of his followers and friends entertained a thought of opposing England. When, in obedience to the popular demand, the old Assembly had been dissolved and newly elected burgesses, favorable to Bacon, had convened, they proposed the redress of "several grievances the country was then laboring under," but they did not give the slightest hint of an intention to "defy" England. Later, in his "Remonstrance" against the governor's proclamation declaring him to be a rebel and a traitor, Bacon declared that he and his followers were loyal subjects of the king and in arms against the Indians only. If we may put faith in what he said, we must conclude that he believed Governor Berkeley to be the real rebel and traitor, who, as the king's official representative, had betrayed his trust, and was using his power contrary to the king's wishes and to the detriment of the king's faithful colony.

Altogether consistent with this belief is "the oath at Middle Plantation," by which Bacon sought to bind his friends, "until such time as the king be fully informed of the state of the case . . . and the determination thereof be remitted hither," to resist any force that the governor might send against him, even though it should consist of English troops. This "oath on the Virginia Field of Mars to fight England," as it has been bombastically styled, was, in the intention of those who subscribed it, nothing more than an expression of their determination to appeal their cases to the king and, until the king's decision was rendered, to resist any force whatever that the governor might send to capture them and hang them as traitors. This was something very different from swearing to fight England, and even this was reluctantly done. Bacon's friends refused to sign the paper at first; and when, by threats, appeals, and a suspiciously timely report that the Indians were on the warpath, they were finally induced to sign it, they did so with the express understanding that it was not intended to bind them to anything inconsistent with their allegiance. Say what we may of "these loyal prime gentlemen, who were so punctilious about their allegiance to the king" and yet took "the oath to fight the king's-troops if they came to Virginia," the facts, fairly considered, show that, whatever may have been the mistakes and inconsistencies into which they were driven by the stress of circumstances, they were not disloyal in spirit and intention.

Referring to the sentiment in Virginia a quarter of a century after Bacon's Rebellion, Cooke says: "The society continues to be English throughout, loyal to the king, and believing in social degrees and the Established Church."

This loyal sentiment was manifested by the Virginians up to and even after the actual beginning of hostilities between England and her American colonies. In the decade preceding the outbreak of hostilities some of them, like Patrick Henry, seemed to be strongly inclined to sever the ties of allegiance that bound them to the mother country; but most of them were still faithful subjects of the king. In 1765, in the House of Burgesses, they received with cries of "Treason" Henry's famous words: "Caesar had his Brutus; Charles the First, his Cromwell; and George the Third may profit by their example." Among those who cried "Treason" there was probably not a man who dissented from the view of colonial rights set forth in the resolutions which Henry was urging the Assembly to adopt; and those who opposed their adoption did so because they believed the times called for action tending to allay rather than excite animosity. They understood their chartered rights fully as well as the fiery young orator did, and were no less determined to maintain them; but, after the fashion of their fathers, they wished to maintain them lawfully and with due regard to their obligations as Englishmen, and they were not disposed to approve expressions of defiance and menace to their king.

Their grievance was not a king, but a Parliament that had unlawfully come between them and the crown and was seeking to deprive them of the self-government granted to their fathers by the crown and held by them as an inalienable heritage. They claimed that the relations of Virginia had been, and still rightfully were, with the crown alone; that the crown, by the charter granted in 1621, had conferred on her people the right to be governed by their own representatives convened as her "General Assembly;" that, therefore, she was lawfully a kingdom ruled by her own Parliament, in constitutional subjection to the king, in the same way that England was; and that the English Parliament had no more right to make laws for her people than her Parliament had to make laws for the English people. It was this infringement of their chartered rights by a legislative body in which they had no representation and the authority of which they did not acknowledge that they were determined to resist. They were loyal subjects of the crown, but they did not intend to become slavish subjects of the British Parliament. What they desired, and but for the hotspurs of the time might possibly have secured, was not separation from England, but self-government as an English kingdom. Few Virginians then wished to break loose from the mother country and set up an independent government. Of the sentiment of the people at that time Cooke says: "The old attachment to what was called 'home' was still exceedingly strong. It had been shaken, but not destroyed, and was still a controlling sentiment. To resist openly the crown would invite coercion; and that meant war, which would be deplorable. Even if the colonies were successful, separation from the mother land would probably follow; and not one Virginian in ten thousand desired such a separation."

In the other Southern colonies, as in Virginia, loyal feeling was strong, and there was little disposition on the part of the people to renounce their allegiance to the crown. Englishmen, with whom the Huguenots rapidly assimilated, were dominant. Dissenters, it is said, outnumbered the adherents of the Church of England; but the evidence goes to show that many, if not most, of the Dissenters were royalist in sentiment. In the history of these colonies we read of the lawlessness and turbulence which are more or less characteristic of all newly settled countries. There were outbreaks of personal enmities, factional fights; violent attempts to redress local grievances, uprisings in resistance to the injustice and oppression of corrupt and tyrannical officials; but through all the better part of the people were ever loyal to the crown.

Of these Southern colonies Lodge says that North Carolina was "an offshoot, in large measure, of the great colony of Virginia," whose "planters closely resembled those of Virginia;" that in South Carolina "the Virginian type of manners and society becomes wholly Southern, while all the essential peculiarities of the Virginian group of colonies are intensified and are not only predominant, but reign alone;" and that in Georgia "there was more loyalty and dependence upon the crown than elsewhere." Doyle says: "The Southern colonies were in full what England always was in part: communities governed by an unpaid aristocracy of wealth and birth." Had there been no influences of blood, tradition, and training binding these Southerners to loyalty, the fact stated by Doyle would doubtless have made them reluctant to renounce their allegiance to the crown; for aristocracy and wealth are naturally conservative—naturally uphold constituted government and the established order of things, and oppose radical and violent measures of reform and progress as dangerous.

But however reluctant the Southerners may have been to sever the political ties that bound them to the mother country, when war was determined on and they were constrained to choose between loyalty to the land of their ancestors and loyalty to the land in which they had made homes for themselves and their children, the great majority of them chose the latter and, with whole-hearted devotion, periled their lives and their fortunes in the long struggle for independence. Their descendants can read with just pride the story of how they acquitted themselves in that struggle.

When the struggle was brought to a successful issue and the colonies, separately and by name, were recognized by Great Britain as independent States, the Southern people gave their undivided allegiance to their respective States. When these States entered into a federal union on the conditions set forth in the Constitution, they felt that loyalty to their States obliged them to be loyal to the terms of the compact. Hence Southern men never spoke of the Constitution with contempt. On the contrary, through the press, from the platform, in the halls of Congress, in the Senate Chamber, always and everywhere they upheld it and clung to it as the palladium of their liberty. They were called "strict constructionists" because they protested against any latitudinarian construction of the Constitution to justify party policies or expedient measures, and insisted that it should be interpreted and obeyed according to its plain meaning and as it was understood by the men who framed it and the States that ratified it. They regarded it as the instrument in which the States had solemnly pledged themselves, each to the others, and the terms of which could not be violated in any manner or degree without dishonor. They faithfully fulfilled the obligations it imposed on them, and insisted on the faithful observance of all its provisions as necessary to the common weal. They freely conceded the rights it granted to others, and asked only that others would concede the rights it granted to them.

When we turn to the history of the Puritans, we read an altogether different story. We find them at first a strictly religious sect, called Puritans in derision because they professed to follow "the pure word of God." They regarded themselves as the "chosen of God," and looked with contempt on the richest, noblest, and best who were not of his chosen company. Their "bond to other men," says Green, "was not the sense of a common manhood, but the recognition of a brotherhood among the elect. Without the pale of the saints lay a world which was hateful to them because it was the enemy of their God." It is, then, no great exaggeration to say that they were "characterized by the Pharisaism that worships itself and is unable to perceive any goodness apart from itself."

Holding that their duty and interests alike required them, under all circumstances, to follow "the pure word," they were determined to obey every command which they believed to be divine, even though it might be to disobey the law of the land or to violate their plighted faith. Thus they were characterized by the spirit that "holds its ideas, its interests, and its will to be higher than fundamental law and covenanted obligations." Many of them unquestionably were, and most of them may have been, honest and sincere. They diligently searched the Scriptures, and followed what they believed to be the divine will revealed therein. Practically they admitted no possibility of error in their understanding of the Scriptures and no possibility of truth in any interpretation at variance with their own. They held their own notion of "the pure word" to be the supreme law, which must be obeyed without the slightest concession.

This was well enough so long as their notion of "the pure word" was held to be the law for the regulation of their own conduct in things religious and pertaining to themselves only, for in all such things every man ought to be obedient to his own idea of what is right. But the Puritans were not content with that. As they gained in numbers and power they entered the political arena and sought forcibly to regulate the affairs of the whole country according to their notion of "the pure word"—forcibly to mold English politics and English religion into accord with their idea of the will of God.

Since the Puritans fought for the Parliament against the king, and since the purpose of the Parliament was to compel the king to exercise his power within constitutional limits, a superficial view of the case might lead to the conclusion that they fought for constitutional government. But their purpose was altogether different from that of the

Parliament; and while it was not openly declared in the beginning, it became clearly evident after Cromwell was placed in command of the army. From that time on they were obedient to Parliament only in so far as it did what they wished it to do. They overthrew the king in the name of the Parliament, and then overthrew the Parliament to effect their own ends.

An English historian, who highly praises them as "a brave, a wise, an honest, and a useful body," says: "In politics the Independents [the Cromwellian Puritans] were, to use the phrase of their time, root and branch men, or, to use the kindred phrase of our own time, radicals. Not content with limiting the power of the monarch, they were desirous to erect a commonwealth on the ruins of the old English polity." To express it a little more plainly, yet in accord with the facts, they were desirous to overthrow the English government and establish in its stead a theocracy under the name of commonwealth, ruled by them as the vicegerents of God, having their idea of the divine will as its supreme law and visiting dire punishment on all who might refuse to obey it. To effect this end they "rebelled against constituted authority," practiced "the most cruel and pitiless tyranny," beheaded the king, oppressed the country, and "trampled upon the rights of others." The king, the Parliament, the law, all things that stood in the way of the accomplishment of their purpose were ruthlessly set aside. They seemed to find a grim pleasure in humiliating superiors, defying authorities, and heaping contempt on things that others regarded as sacred and inviolable.

In telling how they brought about the execution of the king, Macaulay, who seems to have disapproved the deed only because it was inexpedient, says: "And now a design to which at the commencement of the civil war no man would have dared to allude, and which was not less inconsistent with the Solemn League and Covenant than with the old law of England, began to take distinct form. The austere warriors who ruled the nation had during some months meditated a fearful vengeance on the captive king. . . . The military saints resolved that, in defiance of the old laws of the realm and of the almost universal sentiment of the nation, the king should expiate his crimes with his blood. . . . They enjoyed keenly the very scandal which they caused. That the ancient constitution and the public opinion of England were directly opposed to regicide made regicide seem strangely fascinating to a party bent on effecting a complete political and social revolution. In order to accomplish their purpose, it was necessary that they should first break in pieces every part of the machinery of the government; and this necessity was rather agreeable than painful to them. The Commons passed a vote tending to accommodation with the king. The soldiers excluded the majority by force. The Lords unanimously rejected the proposition that the king should be brought to trial. Their house was instantly closed. No court known to the law would take on itself the office of judging the fountain of justice. A revolutionary tribunal was created. That tribunal pronounced Charles a tyrant, a traitor, a murderer, and a public enemy, and his head was severed from his shoulders before thousands of spectators in front of the banqueting hall of his own palace."

Such were the Puritans of England—a religious sect that entered the political arena, overthrew both king and Parliament, and, exulting in their lawlessness, "broke in pieces every part of the machinery of the government;" a political party composed of religious zealots who regarded their idea of right as a law higher than royal decrees, legislative enactments, and constitutional requirements, and, in obedience to that "higher law," set at naught the traditions, customs, and laws of the realm. "The Puritan," says Green, "was bound by his very religion to examine every claim made on his civil and spiritual obedience by the powers that be, and to own or reject the claim as it accorded with the higher duty which he owed to God." He incarnated the spirit that exalts itself above all human laws and follows the dictates of its own judgment in defiance of constituted authorities and regardless of the rights of others.

A little more than twenty years before the outbreak of the civil war in England a small company of these Puritans crossed the Atlantic in the famous Mayflower, landed at Plymouth, and, overcoming obstacles that seemed almost insurmountable, established themselves in the new country. It has been said that "no event in American history has been followed by results more potent in the making of this country than the settlement of the Pilgrims at

Plymouth;" but, as the facts show, the Plymouth colony never exerted any considerable influence, and was finally annexed by the Massachusetts Company, which settled at Salem eight years later. It was this stronger colony that became so influential in shaping the destiny of the country.

These New England Puritans were one in spirit with the Puritan brethren whom they had left in Old England. This spirit was, of course, modified by its new environment and developed along different lines; but it was essentially the same as that which "put its foot on the neck of the king." It was the spirit that sets itself above the law, judges the law, and rebels against any law that does not accord with its judgment.

This spirit of rebellion against law may be traced throughout the history of the New England fathers and their descendants. Palfrey reveals the disloyal temper and intent of those who founded the Massachusetts colony when he says in their defense that "those were not times for such men as the Massachusetts patentees to ask what the king wished or expected, but rather how much of freedom could be maintained against him by the letter of the law or by other righteous means."

They had hardly become comfortably settled in their new home before they began to violate the spirit, if not the letter, of their charter by acts repugnant to the laws of England. Instead of being loyal subjects, they and their descendants during the entire term of their colonial life not only went to the utmost length allowed by the letter of the law in disobedience to the home government, but resisted that government by every illegal expedient which they judged to be safe and good. The deeds for which the children of our country are taught to honor them most highly—such, for example, as the famous "Boston tea party"—were prompted by the spirit of disloyalty and done in defiance of law. It was by such lawless deeds that they precipitated the Revolutionary War — deeds which, whatever of good may have resulted from them and however we may laud them as displaying patriotism and love of liberty, were exhibitions of the old Puritan spirit of rebellion.

This rebellious Puritan spirit continued to manifest itself after the colonies had won their independence and, as independent States, had formed the Union. For many years the men of New England, paying little regard to the government on the other side of the sea, had been doing much as they pleased; and they had become so habituated to having their own way that they found it difficult to fall in gracefully with the ways of others. It has been aptly said: "New England was partial to strong government, but was equally fond of governing." There was the stronghold of the Federalists, who, as Mr. Stephens says, "acted generally upon the principle that the Federal government was a consolidated Union of the people of all the States in one single, great republic," but "still kept the party name of Federal because it was popular." Distrusting the ability of the people to govern themselves, they favored a general government vested with much power, and they also desired to dictate its policy. Indeed, their letters and other documents of the period indicate a belief on their part that they alone were fit to govern, and that, if not governed by them, the country would speedily go to ruin. Hence when Jefferson, representing political principles at variance with their own, was elected to the presidency, and the acquisition of Louisiana threatened permanently to debar their section from dominance, they plotted to form a Northern Confederacy.

A prominent leader in this project was Timothy Pickering, who had been in Washington's cabinet, and who represented Massachusetts in the Senate. The success of Jeffersonian Democracy greatly displeased him and led him to say in a letter to George Cabot, "And shall we sit still until this system shall universally triumph — until even in the Eastern States the principles of genuine Federalism shall be overwhelmed? The principles of our Revolution point to a remedy—a separation. . . . The people of the East cannot reconcile their habits, views, and interests with those of the South and West. ... A Northern Confederacy would unite congenial characters and present a fairer prospect of public happiness; while the Southern States, having a similarity of habits, might be left to manage their own affairs in their own way."

Similar views were entertained by Governor Roger Griswold, of Connecticut, who, in a letter (March 11, 1804) to Oliver Wolcott, said: "I have no hesitation myself in saying that there can be no safety to the Northern States without a separation from the confederacy. [confederacy here means the confederation or "union" of the United States of

America.] The balance of power under the present government is decidedly in favor of the Southern States; nor can that balance be changed or destroyed. The question, then, is, Can it be safe to remain under a government in whose measures we can have no effective agency?

The project which we had formed was to induce, if possible, the legislatures of the three New England States who remain Federal to commence measures which should call for a reunion of the Northern States."

> ANNOTATION: Roger Griswold was the 22nd governor of Connecticut, who lived from 1762 until 1812. His father was Matthew Griswold, the 17th governor of Connecticut. With widespread approval in his home state, Roger Griswold was stalwartly against the war with Great Britain. He refused to allow the Connecticut militia to be under the command of the federal government. The subsequent constitutional debates continued after Griswold's death on October 25, 1812.
>
> (See the entire letter in "Documents Relating to New-England Federalism: 1800-1815," by John Quincy Adams, edited by Henry Adams, Boston: Little, Brown and Company, 1905, pages 354-358.)

That such a "reunion of the Northern States" was desired by more than "a little knot of politicians," is clearly indicated by a letter from Judge Reeve to Senator Tracy, in which the writer said: "I have seen many of our friends, and all that I have seen, and most that I have heard from, believe that we must separate, and that this is the most favorable moment. ... I have heard of only three gentlemen as yet who appear undecided upon this subject." But Cabot, Ames, and others, while favoring the idea of separation, thought it impracticable at that time, as the people did not then "feel the necessity of it." "The separation will be unavoidable," wrote Cabot, "when our loyalty is perceived to be the instrument of impoverishment."

Because of the timidity of some and the jealousy of others enlisted in it, and because of the failure of the plot to make Burr Governor of New York and swing that State into line with it, the project to form a Northern Confederacy came to naught; but the fact remains that the political leaders of New England plotted to take the Northern States out of the Union.

These men could not claim, as the Southern people could, that they had been, or probably would be, deprived of any rights guaranteed to them by the Federal compact. Their only ground of complaint was that the people had not indorsed their idea of government, that their political party had been defeated, that Jeffersonian Democracy had triumphed, and that they had lost power. John Quincy Adams described them as "a faction which has succeeded in obtaining the management of this commonwealth, and which aspired to the government of the Union. Defeated in this last object of their ambition and sensible that the engines by which they had attained the mastery of the State 'were not sufficiently comprehensive nor enough within their control to wield the machinery of the nation, their next resort was to dismember what they could not sway and to form a new confederacy, to be under the glorious shelter of British protection."

A few years after the failure of this project to form a Northern Confederacy New England was in still more pronounced rebellion against the Federal government. When Great Britain was enforcing unjust restrictions on American trade; when English war vessels were lying in wait to overhaul American merchantmen; when American seamen were being outraged and impressed, and American ships were being seized and sold; when the country's maritime and commercial rights and the liberties of her citizens were assailed and every effort to secure them by peaceable means had failed; when, as President Madison said, there was actually "on the side of Great Britain a state of war against the United States," and nothing short of a resort to arms by this country could satisfy the demands of national honor and protect the national interests, Congress authorized the President to call out the militia of the States and formally declared war.

As soon as war was declared, New England Federalists began to concert measures to hinder the government in its prosecution. The men who, while efforts were being made to secure the country's rights by negotiation, had jeered at the administration as "incapable of being kicked into war," now vehemently denounced the administration for plunging the country into a "needless war." Mr. Clay said of them: "They are for war and no restrictions when the administration is for peace. They are for peace and restrictions when the administration is for war. You find them, sir, tacking with every gale, steady only in one unalterable purpose—to steer, if possible, into the haven of power." They promptly took steps in opposition to the government's policy. The Federalists in Congress, in an address to the people of New England, protested against the war as unnecessary and unwise. The Massachusetts House of Representatives declared that it was opposed to the interests of New England, called for town meetings fearlessly and strongly to express disapprobation of it, and urged that there should be "no volunteers except for defensive war." The Supreme Court of Massachusetts denied the right of the President or Congress to determine the conditions under which State militia may be called into the service of the United States, and affirmed that such right belonged to the governor only. The governor refused the President's request for the State's quota of militia, and proclaimed a public fast because of the declaration of war "against a nation from which we are descended, and which for many generations has been the bulwark of the religion we profess."

Every possible influence—legal, financial, social, and religious—was exerted to prevent men from enlisting or loaning money to the government. Laws were passed to embarrass recruiting officers. Enlisted men were arrested on real or fictitious charges of indebtedness and prevented from leaving the State. Citizens were threatened with public contempt and financial loss if they loaned money to the government. "It is very grateful to find," said the Boston Gazette, "that the universal sentiment is that any man who lends his money to the government at the present time will forfeit all claim to common honesty and common courtesy among all true friends of the country. God forbid that any Federalist should ever hold up his hand to pay Federalists for money lent to the present rulers; and Federalists can judge whether Democrats will tax their constituents to pay interest to Federalists." The New England clergy thundered against the war, heaped abuse on its "authors," and pronounced the curse of God on all who in any way aided in its prosecution. Some idea of the eloquence that flowed from the New England pulpits of those days may be gathered from the following sample, extracted from the outpourings of Rev. Mr. Osgood at Medford, Massachusetts: "If at the command of weak or wicked rulers they undertake an unjust war, each man who volunteers his services in such a cause or loans money for its support or by his conversation, his writings, or any other mode of influence encourages its prosecution—that man is an accomplice in the wickedness, loads his conscience with the blackest crimes, brings the guilt of blood upon his soul, and in the sight of God and his law is a murderer. Were not the authors of this war in character nearly akin to the deists and atheists of France? Were they not men of hardened hearts, seared consciences, reprobate minds, and desperate wickedness? It seems utterly inconceivable that they should have made the declaration."

In his eagerness to save the members of his flock from the heinous crime of aiding their own countrymen, the New England shepherd apparently neglected to warn them against the sin of "giving aid and comfort to the enemy." They furnished the British troops with greatly needed supplies, and thereby put much British gold into their own pockets. It was largely on the provisions furnished by New England that the British army in Canada subsisted.

New England money, as well as New England provisions, went to aid the enemy. Boston banks, which, instead of helping, tried financially to cripple the United States government, paid millions for British government bills. In the *Olive Branch*, Matthew Carey said: "That these bills to an immoderate amount were transmitted from Quebec, that they were drawn for the support of the armies employed in hostilities against the country, that they were paid for in specie devoted to the support of those armies, are facts too stubborn to be set aside." Mr. Carey claimed to have specific proof of these charges, and publicly defied any man in the Union to refute them. And while millions were being paid for British government bills, no citizen of Massachusetts could let it be known that he had taken any part of his own government's loans without bringing upon himself the denunciations of the pulpit and press and the condemnation of the people generally.

Throughout the war New England was practically in rebellion. Her people sympathized with and aided Great Britain, heard with satisfaction of British successes, and deplored American victories. When loyal citizens were rejoicing because of the capture of the Peacock by Captain Lawrence, Josiah Quincy reported and the Senate of Massachusetts adopted a preamble and resolution opposing a vote of thanks to Lawrence on the ground that it might be considered "as an encouragement and excitement to the continuance of the present unjust, unnecessary, and iniquitous war," and declaring that "it is not becoming a moral and religious people to express any approbation of military or naval exploits which are not immediately connected with the defense of our seacoast and soil."

The Salem Gazette plainly revealed its sympathy with the enemy by thus announcing Harrison's victory over Proctor: "At length the handful of British troops, which for more than a year have baffled the numerous armies of the United States in the invasion of Canada, have been obliged to yield to superior power and numbers." Harrison's victory was designated by one New England journal as "the triumph of a crowd of Kentucky savages over a handful of brave men."

It is evident that the ultra-Federalists desired to see the American army vanquished and the American flag lowered in defeat in order that the political party then in power might be brought into disrepute. The facts clearly prove that they conspired to reduce the country to such straits, create such widespread dissatisfaction, and bring the administration into such discredit as would enable them either to get control of the government or, failing in that, take the Northern States out of the Union. In legislative halls, in newspapers, and from the pulpit this was substantially avowed.

At what seemed to them a propitious time the Massachusetts Federalists, in keeping with their design to control or dismember the Union, by a three to one vote of the State legislature called for a convention of the States concurring in the belief that the Constitution of the United States had failed of its purpose, that the provisions for its amendment were inadequate, and that it therefore devolved on the people to take such steps as their safety demanded. In response to this call the famous Hartford Convention met on December 15, 1814. It was composed of delegates appointed by the legislatures of Massachusetts, Connecticut, and Rhode Island, and representatives, not thus formally appointed, from New Hampshire and Vermont.

This Convention declared, "A severance of the Union by one or more States, against the will of the rest and especially in time of war, can be justified only by absolute necessity. . . . But in cases of deliberate, dangerous, and palpable infractions of the Constitution, affecting the sovereignty of a State and the liberties of the people, it is not only the right, but the duty of such a State to interpose its authority for their protection in the manner best calculated to secure that end. When emergencies occur which are either beyond the reach of the judicial tribunals or too pressing to admit of the delay incident to their forms, States which have no common umpire must be their own judges and execute their own decisions."

After thus asserting the "right" and "duty" of a State to withdraw from the Union when, in its judgment, such action may be necessary to protect its "sovereignty" and "the liberties of the people," the Convention recommended that the legislatures of the States represented therein should adopt and persevere in their efforts to obtain certain sweeping amendments of the Constitution of the United States;

that they should pass laws authorizing the governors to make detachments from the militia or form voluntary corps and "cause the same to be well armed, equipped, and disciplined, and held in readiness for service;" that they should request the government of the United States to empower the said States, "separately or in concert, to assume upon themselves the defense of their territory," and to appropriate therefor a portion of the revenue raised within them; and that, in case of the failure of their application to the government, another convention should be held, "with such powers and instructions as the exigency of a crisis so momentous may require."

Stripped of circumlocutions and boiled down, the proceedings of the Hartford Convention, so far as they are known, amount to about this: "We, the States herein represented, assert that it is our right and duty to withdraw from the Union if in our judgment such a step should be necessary to our protection. We recommend such changes and ask such concessions as we judge to be necessary to protect us; and in case of the government's refusal to grant what we ask, we will hold another convention and take such steps as we may deem necessary to protect ourselves." The inference that they intended to secede from the Union and form a new confederacy if the government refused to submit to their dictation is too plain to be avoided.

The legislatures of Massachusetts and Connecticut appointed commissioners to proceed to Washington and submit the Convention's demands to the government; but the news of Jackson's victory at New

Orleans and the treaty of peace signed at Ghent completely changed the situation, and the demand on the government was never made. The commissioners returned home as quietly as possible, and in the general rejoicing caused by the successful issue of the war the public indignation excited by the conduct of New England gave place to good humor.

The rebellion of New England in the War of 1812 was far more shameful than anything that her bitterest enemy can charge against the South. Never did a Southern State officially condemn the Federal government for declaring a war which could not be averted by honorable means. Never did a Southern State refuse to respond loyally to the call of the government for its quota of men to uphold the honor and maintain the rights of the country. Never did a Southern State turn against the government in its hour of need and give aid and comfort to its enemies. The South openly and boldly contended for what she believed to be her unquestionable right, and fired on the old flag when it was unfurled with hostile intent in her own territory and was waving over an army invading her soil to deprive her States of their independence and reduce them, in fact if not in name, to the condition of subject provinces; but never did she, either by refusing aid to those upholding it or by giving aid to its enemies, attempt to lower that flag in defeat when it was unfurled against a foreign foe. In the New England rebellion there was no open, courageous, and manly assertion of rights that were threatened; no sacrifice of material interests to maintain a cherished principle; no display of high and disinterested patriotism; not a single redeeming feature unless it be that the war was really opposed to her notion of right, and that, after the manner of her rebellious Puritan ancestors, she held her notion of right to be above her allegiance to her government and her obligations to the other States.

Some of New England's sons deeply and keenly felt the disgrace of their States and bitterly arraigned those who were responsible for it. Among these was John Holmes, who had been a Federalist, but had left that party when he perceived its "rule or ruin" policy. In the Massachusetts Senate he said, "Afraid to overthrow the Constitution, you try to undermine it by pretense of amendment. You called it perfect while you were in pay. The friends of peace, declaring that the country could not be kicked into war, forced it on, and, failing to repossess themselves of the administration, tried to destroy the government. An unauthorized and unconstitutional assemblage at Hartford is to change a Constitution declared unfit for war or peace, but which you dare not attack openly." And again, "You boast of forbearance, but you forbore only because you were afraid to go further. You complain of Southern aggrandizement with ten members in the Senate—an undue proportion according to your population. Massachusetts has become contemptible, a byword of reproach. Your conduct has disgusted the people everywhere."

It is a mistake to suppose that, "with this wretched display of treachery, Federalism vanished forever from American politics." Its body—the political organization calling itself the Federal party— was killed; but its rebellious soul, like that of John Brown, kept "marching on." It only burrowed deeper and worked more assiduously. Mr. Jefferson, with clear and prophetic political vision notwithstanding his advanced age, perceived its presence in the controversy about the admission of Missouri to statehood and foretold its purpose. In a letter to General Dearborn regarding the Missouri question Jefferson said:

> I see only that it has given resurrection to the Hartford Convention men ... Desperate of regaining power under political distinctions, they have adroitly wriggled into its seat under the auspices of morality, and are again in the ascendency from which their sins had hurled them.

To William Pinkney he wrote:

> The Missouri question is a mere party trick. The leaders of Federalism, defeated in their schemes of obtaining power by rallying partisans to the principle of monarchism—a principle of personal, not of local, division— have changed their tack and thrown out another barrel to the whale. They are taking advantage of the virtuous feelings of the people to effect a division of parties by a geographical line. They expect that this will insure them, on local principles, the majority they could never obtain on principles of Federalism.

Writing to Lafayette on the same subject, he said:

> It is not a moral question, but one merely of power. Its object is to raise a geographical principle for the choice of a President, and the noise will be kept up till that is effected. All know that permitting the slaves of the South to spread into the West will not add one being to that unfortunate condition; that it will increase the happiness of those existing; and, by spreading them over a larger

surface, will dilute the evil everywhere and facilitate the means of finally getting rid of it—an event more anxiously wished by those on whom it presses than by the noisy pretenders to exclusive humanity. In the meantime it is a ladder for rivals climbing to power.

Hildreth, in his "History of the United States," virtually admits that the agitation of the slavery question in connection with the admission of Missouri to statehood had its origin and purpose in the desire of the Federalists to effect Northern supremacy and place themselves in power. He says, "Jealousy of Southern domination had, as we have seen, made the Northern Federalists dissatisfied with the purchase of Louisiana. It had led them to protest against the erection of the territory of Orleans into a State, and had moved the Hartford Convention to propose the abolition of the slave representation. The keeping out of new States or the alteration of the Constitution as to the basis of representation were projects too hopeless as well as too unpopular in their origin to be renewed. The extension to the new territory west of the Mississippi of the ordinance of 1787 against slavery seemed to present a much more feasible method of accomplishing substantially the same object. This idea, spreading with rapidity, still further obliterated old party ties, tending to produce at the North a political union for which the Federalists had so often sighed."

Thus Federalism, instead of "vanishing from American politics" with its "wretched display of treachery" during the War of 1812, merely disguised itself in the garb of morality and adopted new means to accomplish its purpose. Cloaking its real object under the profession of conscientious opposition to slavery, it now posed before the people not as the advocate of monarchical principles, but as the devoted friend of the slave and the righteous advocate of universal freedom. Its opposition to slavery, however, was always such as tended to excite sectional feeling and further its political ends rather than such as tended to the discovery and adoption of wise and pacific means of ameliorating and ultimately eradicating the evil which so offended its conscience. Through it all could be detected more hate for the Southern whites than love for the Southern blacks, a desire to humiliate the slave owner stronger than the desire to liberate the slave.

In due time it organized its forces into the Republican party, which was, in reality, the old Federal party resurrected, masquerading under the name of the party that had defeated it in the beginning of the century and using the widespread sentiment against slavery as a stepping-stone to political power and control.

This party plainly showed the earmarks of the old New England Federalists. It was no whit behind them in claiming superior wisdom and virtue, in abusing and slandering the men of the South, in speaking of the Constitution as unworthy of respect and obedience unless construed in accordance with its ideas, in refusing to obey the laws of the land that its righteous judgment did not approve, and in practically asserting for itself the right "to decide above the nation and for the nation."

The antislavery element in this party was composed, for the most part, of men who contemplated their own enlightenment and righteousness with the utmost complacency; thanked God that they were not as the ignorant, wicked, and barbarous slave owners of the South; and felt, or professed to feel, that they were divinely called to extirpate the evil of slavery. Like the Puritans who followed Cromwell, they were "root and branch" men, bent on doing their work of extirpation thoroughly, in defiance of law and regardless of constitutional provisions. If the Constitution did not accord with their views and purposes, they held it to be "a covenant with death and an agreement with hell," which all honest and godly men should regard with contempt. They made their conscience the supreme law not only for themselves, but for the whole country; and in their determination to compel obedience to it they rebelled against all obligations and restraints imposed by the government.

That such was their rebellious temper is evidenced by the speeches of their representative men, the acts of legislatures controlled by them, the resolutions adopted in their mass meetings, their refusal to obey the law, and their openly avowed approval of lawless acts.

Northern speakers, engaged in propagating antislavery sentiment, very plainly taught that the patriotic citizen should set his individual judgment of the country's duty to God and mankind above the law which expressed the public judgment of that duty and obey no law which his judgment did not approve—a rule of action which, if generally adopted, would result in anarchy. Of course these speakers did not mean that this rule of action should be followed in all cases; but they did mean, and were understood to mean, that it should be applied to the Federal laws relating to slavery. It was with reference to the Federal law for carrying out the constitutional provision for the return of fugitive slaves that Mr. George William Curtis said: "The name of law has always been the glove muffled in which the hand of Tyranny has taken Liberty by the throat. . . . You are not to suppose that a law is, under all circumstances, to be obeyed; you would be poor children of seven years' armed disobedience to laws if you believed that."

Speaking to the same effect, another distinguished champion of abolition said, "Men say it is anarchy, that the right of the individual to sit in judgment cannot be trusted. It is the lesson of Puritanism. If the individual criticising law cannot be trusted, then Puritanism is a mistake; for the sanctity of individual judgment is the lesson of Massachusetts history in 1620 and 1630. We accepted anarchy as the safest." Set your individual judgment above the judgment of the country as expressed in the laws, and refuse to obey any law that your individual judgment does not approve, was substantially the teaching that issued from the Republican platform and press throughout the North.

The Puritan conscience, deeming itself higher than the Constitution, refused obedience to the "barbarous" and "inhuman" law for the rendition of fugitive slaves. Such a law had been altogether humane, just, and right in 1643, when the first fugitive slave law enacted in America was incorporated into Articles of Confederation formed for mutual benefit by the colonies of Massachusetts, Plymouth, Connecticut, and New Haven; for then New England herself held slaves, and her conscience was blinded by a considerate regard to her own interest, as it has too often been. But when this blinding influence was removed, when she could no longer be profited by the return of fugitive slaves, and only the interest of cruel Southern slave owners was involved, such a law became a moral monstrosity and her enlightened and tender Puritan conscience revolted at it. Throughout the North mass meetings were held in which the people denounced the law and declared their determination to resist all attempts to enforce it. Daniel Webster characterized the resolutions adopted by one of these meetings as "distinctly treasonable," and said of them generally: "In the North the purpose of overturning the government shows itself more clearly in resolutions, agreed to in voluntary assemblies of individuals, denouncing the laws of the land and declaring a fixed intent to disobey them."

The legislatures of most of the Northern States fell into line with the "treasonable" resolutions of the mass meetings and passed no less treasonable laws, making the clause of the Constitution and the acts of Congress, in relation to the rendition of fugitive slaves, inoperative and void. The law of Vermont made any attempt to carry out that provision of the Constitution a penal offense, for which one might be fined as much as ten thousand dollars and imprisoned for twenty years. Think of the loyalty of a State that made it an offense, punishable by a heavy fine and long imprisonment, to obey the law of the land and attempt to carry out a provision of the Constitution of the United States. As Dr. Curry said: "It is a singular political nemesis that nullification and rebellion as terms of reproach should attach to the South, while the North has escaped any odium attaching to the terms, although she openly and successfully nullified the Constitution, and the flag of rebellion against the Federal compact and Federal laws floated over half her capitols."

Not content with resisting the enforcement of the law in their own States, Northern men attempted to destroy the peace and tranquillity of the Southern States. The Puritan conscience, which was so tender that it could not consent to the return of a fugitive slave to his master in obedience to law, could find nothing to shock its sensitiveness in unlawful attempts to incite the slave to put a torch to his master's house and a dagger in his master's heart. John Brown went into Virginia to convert the peaceful homes of that law-abiding commonwealth into scenes of conflagration, outrage, and murder. He was arrested, tried, convicted, and executed according to law. In glowing eulogies Northern men applauded his act, represented him as a saintly hero and martyr whose example should be followed, and characterized as brutal despots those who legally punished his atrocious crime. In an address before the Congregational Society at Boston Wendell Phillips extolled him as a glorious exponent of the "Puritan principle," and said: "He went down to Virginia, took possession of a town, and held it. He says, 'You thought this was strength; I demonstrate it is weakness. You thought this was civil society; I show you it is a den of pirates.' Then he turned around in his sublimity, with his Puritan devotional heart, and said to the millions: 'Learn!' And God lifted a million hearts to his gibbet, as the Roman cross lifted a million hearts to it in that divine sacrifice of two thousand years ago. To-day, more than a statesman could have taught in seventy years, one act of a week has taught eighteen millions of people. That is the Puritan 'principle. What shall it teach us? 'Go thou and do likewise.' Do it by a resolute life; do it by a fearless rebuke; do it by preaching the sermon of which this act is the text; do it by standing by the great example which God has given us; do it by tearing asunder the veil of respectability which covers brutality calling itself law."

This was the spirit dominating the North in 1860. It was not the spirit of a majority of the Northern people, but it was the spirit of a fanatical minority that dominated the country, just as it was the spirit of a fanatical minority that dominated England when Charles I. was beheaded. The spirit that moved John Brown and those who glorified him was marching through the Northern States, contemning the Constitution, defying the laws, inciting to crime, and preparing the way for the overthrow of the government established by the fathers of the republic.

And, like the Puritans who followed Cromwell, these Northern rebels seemed to find a ferocious pleasure in resorting to lawlessness in order, as they said, to rouse those who "still slumbered in submission to law;" and in defying government in order, as they said, to expose the "tyranny" hidden under it. They exulted in their treason, and seemed to think it an evidence of their superior enlightenment and more exalted virtue. "Thanks to God," said Wendell Phillips, "a Hunker cannot live in Massachusetts without being wider awake than he imagines. He must imbibe fanaticism. Insurrection is epidemic in the State; treason is our inheritance. The Puritans planted it in the very structure of the State."

> ANNOTATION: The word "Hunker," meant a member of the conservative faction in the Democratic Party. Phillips is saying, in essence, in order to live in Massachusetts, a conservative must become a radical.

No Southern State can boast of such an inheritance. In whole-hearted loyalty to the government as it was established by the fathers; in unfailing fidelity to the Constitution as it was construed by the men who framed it and understood by the States that adopted it; in unswerving devotion to the Union which was founded on that Constitution and recognized the sovereignty and political equality of the federated States; in magnanimous sacrifices of her own interest to promote the public good; in patriotic responses to the country's calls for men and money to maintain her rights, carry out her policies, and defend her honor; in respect for the legal and moral rights of all men, bond and free; in holding unsullied honor above selfish gain; in fulfilling obligations unto the uttermost; in keeping plighted faith at whatever cost; in redeeming the spoken promise as though it were a written bond; in all social and moral virtues and all manly qualities; in all things commonly held by civilized men to be honorable and praiseworthy, perhaps the South may rightly claim to be the equal of New England. But in fanaticism, insurrection, treason, and other such proud distinctions, inherited or imbibed, she is compelled to admit that New England far surpasses her.

APPENDIX

A New Yorker's poem insulting the American flag on occasion when the government protected the rights of Southerners by upholding the Fugitive Slave Act.

HAIL TO THE STARS AND STRIPES.

Hail to the Stars and Stripes!
The boastful flag all hail!
The tyrant trembles now,
And at the sight grows pale;
The Old World groans in pain,
And turns her eye to see,
Beyond the Western Main,
The emblem of the Free.
Hail to the Stars and Stripes!
Hope beams in every ray!
And, shining through the bars
Of gloom, points out the way;
The Old World sees the light
That shall her cells illume;
And shrinking back to night,
Oppression reads her doom.
Hail to the Stars and Stripes!
They float in every sea;
The crystal waves speed on,
The emblem of the Free!
Beneath the azure sky
Of soft Italians clime,
Or where Auroras die

In solitude sublime.
All hail the flaunting Lie!
The Stars grow pale and dim—
The Stripes are bloody scars,
A lie the flaunting hymn!
It shields the pirate's deck,
It binds a man in chains;
It yokes the captive's neck,
And wipes the bloody stains.
Tear down the flaunting Lie!
Half-mast the starry flag!
Insult no sunny sky
With Hate's polluted rag!
Destroy it, ye who can!
Deep sink it in the waves!
It bears a fellow man
To groan with fellow slaves!
Awake the burning scorn!
The vengeance long and deep,
That till a better morn
Shall neither tire nor sleep!
Swear once again the vow,
O freeman! dare to do'.
God's will is ever now!
May His thy will renew!
Unfurl the boasted Lie!
Till freedom lives again,
To reign once more in truth,
Among untrammeled men!
Roll up the starry sheen—
Conceal its bloody stains;
For in its folds are seen

The stamp of rusting chains.
Be bold, ye heroes all!
Spurn, spurn the flaunting Lie,
Till Peace, and Truth, and Love
Shall fill the bending sky;
Then floating in the air,
O'er hill, and dale, and sea,
It will stand forever fair,
The emblem of the Free!

—by Charles Graham Halpine, written for the *New York Herald,* 1854, expressing disgust with the Federal government for enforcing the Fugitive Slave Law.

THE CONQUERED BANNER

By Abram Joseph Ryan, (1838-1886)

Furl that Banner, for 'tis weary;
Round its staff 'tis drooping dreary;
Furl it, fold it, it is best;
For there's not a man to wave it,
And there's not a sword to save it,
And there's no one left to lave it
In the blood that heroes gave it;
And its foes now scorn and brave it;
Furl it, hide it — let it rest!

Take that banner down! 'Tis tattered;
Broken is its shaft and shattered;
And the valiant hosts are scattered

Over whom it floated high.
Oh! 'Tis hard for us to fold it;
Hard to think there's none to hold it;
Hard that those who once unrolled it
Now must furl it with a sigh.

Furl that banner! Furl it sadly!
Once ten thousands hailed it gladly.
And ten thousands wildly, madly,
Swore it should forever wave;
Swore that foeman's sword should never
Hearts like theirs entwined dissever,
Till that flag should float forever
O'er their freedom or their grave!

Furl it! For the hands that grasped it,
And the hearts that fondly clasped it,
Cold and dead are lying low;
And that Banner--it is trailing!
While around it sounds the wailing
Of its people in their woe.

For, though conquered, they adore it!
Love the cold, dead hands that bore it!
Weep for those who fell before it!
Pardon those who trailed and tore it!
But, oh! Wildly they deplored it!
Now who furl and fold it so.

Furl that Banner! True, 'tis gory,
Yet 'tis wreathed around with glory,
And 'twill live in song and story,

Though its folds are in the dust;
For its fame on brightest pages,
Penned by poets and by sages,
Shall go sounding down the ages--
Furl its folds though now we must.

Furl that banner, softly, slowly!
Treat it gently--it is holy--
For it droops above the dead.
Touch it not--unfold it never,
Let it droop there, furled forever,
For its people's hopes are dead!

HOW THE CONQUERED BANNER CAME TO BE WRITTEN — AND WAS ALMOST LOST.

FATHER RYAN: "I was in Knoxville when the news came that Gen. Lee had surrendered at Appomattox Court-House. It was night, and I was sitting in my room in a house where many of the regiment of which I was chaplain were quartered, when an old comrade came in and said to me, "All is lost, Gen. Lee has surrendered." I looked at him. I knew by his whitened face that the news was too true. I simply said, "Leave me," and he went out of the room. I bowed my head upon the table and wept long and bitterly. When a thousand thoughts came rushing through my brain. I could not control them. That banner was conquered; its folds must be furled, but its story had to be told. We were very poor in the days of the war. I looked around for a piece of paper to give expression to the thoughts that cried out within me. All that I could find

was a piece of brown wrapping paper from an old pair of shoes that a friend sent me. I seized this piece of paper and wrote the "Conquered Banner" Then I went to bed, leaving the lines there upon the table. The next morning the regiment was ordered away, and I thought no more of the lines written in such sorrow and desolation of spirit on that fateful night. What was my astonishment a few weeks later to see them appear above my name in a Louisville paper! The poor woman who kept the house in Knoxville had gone, as she afterward told me, into the room to throw the piece of paper into the fire, when she saw that there was something written upon it. She said that she sat down and cried, and, copying the lines, she sent them to a newspaper in Louisville. And that was how the 'Conquered Banner' got into print."
Source of information:

http://www.electricscotland.com/History/america/civilwar/conquered_banner.htm

Upon reading this account of the origin of the "Conquered Banner," Mrs. J. William Jones, wife of the Confederate Chaplain-General, and a fervent Confederate from the spring of 1861 when she buckled her husband's armour upon him and sent him to the front down to the present day, wrote these lines:

HOW FATHER RYAN'S "CONQUERED BANNER" WAS RESCUED FROM OBLIVION: BY MRS. J. WILLIAM JONES.

He shared their every hardship, as he did their hopes and joys,
Inspiring faith and courage as he cheered those ragged boys.
Our soldier-priest and poet stood unflinching at his post,
Till the news of Lee's surrender told the story: "All is lost."

He could bare his breast to bayonet, be torn with shot and shell:
With victorious, tattered banner, he could bleed and die so well.
But when those dreadful words, "All lost," broke o'er him like a flood,
His very heart seemed weeping, and his tears all stained with blood.

How illy could he bear it all, so sudden was the blight,
Glut for the poet's genius, which filled his soul with light.
He sought in vain material his burning words to give
To future generations, and to hearts where he would live.

A crushed brown paper on the floor served then his purpose well.

For though it seemed a conquered cause, he must its story tell.
He wrote it out and fell asleep: next morn thought of it not.
New troubles filled the poet's heart — his poem was forgot.

The morning dawned: that broken priest, but soldier never —
Was gone, but left, all blurred with tears that paper on the floor.
A woman, loving well our cause, found, and its folds unfurled,
The "Conquered Banner," and it floats unconquered to the world.
At last he bivouacs in peace: no monument stands guard
To point us where the poet-priest sleeps sweetly 'neath the sod.
His glorious rhythmic poems rare a monument will stand;
He was its architect, and built both gracefully and grand:

Mrs. J. William Jones,
Miller School, Virginia, August 9, 1897

Virginia Sailors and Soldiers Monument, Libby Prison Park, Richmond, Virginia.

Made in the USA
Middletown, DE
05 March 2024